To George,

I believe you will fi[illegible]
Father's book is a wonderfu[illegible]
as you embark into the m[illegible]
of Trout fishing. He was blessed [illegible]
gift to express in the written word [illegible]
many of us feel about this great spor[illegible]

I was fortunate to have shared so many
of the experiences he wrote about.

My Dad would be pleased, as am I,
to share "Grandpa Trout" with you.

Sincerely,

Lloyd

2001

GRANDPA TROUT

GRANDPA TROUT

By

HARRY EDWARD JONES

Prepared for publication
by
Mark Edward Jones

MP

1988

Marker Publishing
Birmingham, Michigan

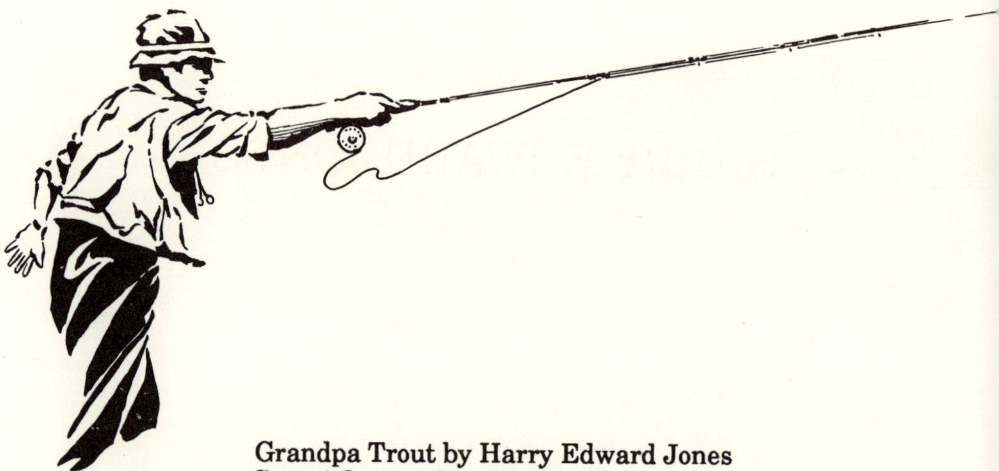

Grandpa Trout by Harry Edward Jones

Library of Congress Catalog Card Number
87-092214

ISBN 0-9619927-0-0

First Edition
Printed in the United States of America

Dedicated to the Memory of

Harry Edward Jones
1903 – 1982

Outdoorsman, Poet, Common Man
Author of
Rhymes of a Common Man and *Grandpa Trout*

Table of Contents

Prelude

I'll pen a line to the towering pine,
With its branches raised in prayer.
A stanza, too, to those lakes of blue,
Cloaked in beauty beyond compare.
To the dew-flecked ferns as the sun returns,
To herald a brand new day.
To the songbird's trill and the oak-treed hill,
With the forest folk at play.

To the winding stream and the angler's dream,
Of the rainbow's rise and swirl.
To a placid sky where the clouds drift by,
In billow of ambered pearl.
To those stately trees of my reveries,
Born in nature's garden fair.
There's a million themes for my penciled dreams,
With a million more to spare.

To the setting sun when the evening's come,
And the night bird's plaintive call.
To the trails I've trod, and a gracious God,
The Creator of them all.

Introduction

A Poet's Prayer

Lord, lend me a descriptive line,
To depict each great creation,
The earth, the seas, the stately trees,
Every God-like innovation.
Just what words describe the rainbow,
In the wake of summer's rain?
What line explains the harvest time,
And those fields of golden grain?

How might I describe the sunrise,
With the freshness of the dew?
Or the glory of the sunset,
Bathed in iridescent hue?
Could I but explain the beauty,
Of each bloom on slender stem,
And those colors you selected,
Ere you laid a brush on them.

How might I write of eventide,
And the moonbeam's peaceful glow,
With the scent of pine logs burning,
In some woodland tableau?
Or a rustic forest setting,
Where a brook goes winding through,
While ensnaring and reflecting,
Every wondrous forest hue?

There's the colors of the songbirds,
And the notes you have them sing,
To awaken buds and blossoms,
To the ecstasies of spring.
The graceful doe and mottled fawn,
'Neath the shadow of the pine,
A scene far beyond the scope,
Of the poet's penciled line.

The colors of the autumn leaves,
The way that you arrange them,
As I seek some descriptive phrase,
To more loveliness you change them.
This natural world of splendor,
Molded to your specific plan,
Give me eloquence befitting,
That I may tell my fellow man.

Preface

A Toast

Here's to the brook and the rainbow,
And a toast to the mighty brown,
To wonderful thrills they've brought me,
While angling both upstream and down.
Here's to the Quill and the Coachman,
May they float in majestic pride,
Here's to the song of the winding stream,
And those memories stored up inside.

Harry Edward Jones

Welcome to the world of *Grandpa Trout*. If you are one of the brotherhood of trout fishermen, you have visited this world often and will find scenes you may well recognize from your own experience. If you have not donned a pair of waders and entered a beautiful stream with rod and reel to spend several quiet hours in peaceful pursuit of the wily trout, then I hope *Grandpa Trout* will help you understand the attraction this pastime has for people of all ages.

Harry Edward Jones was my grandfather, a man whose time on this earth was well spent. He was one of those remarkable people who had a very clear perspective on what is important in life. Born in rural French Quebec, Canada, Grandpa was, for the most part, self-educated. His poetry and stories reflect an intuitive understanding of the world of nature and the actions of men who steal away from cities, jobs, and the cares of everyday life to spend their free time along a meandering stream or in the outdoor cathedral of a pine forest.

Just as a business has its fiscal year, Grandpa's annual trout fishing pilgrimage to northern Michigan was the focus of his year. The significant difference is that Grandpa counted his wealth not in dollars, but in memories of great experiences shared with his companions in, as he often wrote, the "Eden-like beauty of Mother Nature."

It was the rule in our family that you had to be five years old to go with Grandpa on his fishing trip. I was truly fortunate to share in many annual cycles of anticipation and preparation leading up to the great event. In this outdoor school in the company of men, I learned a great many things about life that in middle age I am only now starting to fully appreciate.

Over the years that I participated in the trout fishing pilgrimages, we set up our camp on many different lakes and streams. And on some trips we experienced much better fishing than on others. But even at an early age I came to understand that the lake or stream just provided the backdrop and that fishing just provided the excuse for a trip. These annual excursions were really more about being together and enjoying the beauty and solace of forest and stream.

Of course we did have favorite spots. The river that we frequented most and is so vivid in my memories of early youth is the section of the upper Manistee that flows through Crawford County. And I must admit the trips were always more exciting when the trout were hitting.

While I, and many others of you, have enjoyed the experiences and feelings expressed in *Grandpa Trout*, my grandfather took the time to write them down for us to share. It was not that he thought of himself as a great poet; rather he wanted others to view the great world around us as he did. I think his reason for writing is clear in "A Poet's Prayer," where he asks God to "Give me eloquence befitting, that I may tell my fellow man."

My grandfather's clear and simple style does speak eloquently about his love and respect for the majesty of nature, and the unspoken bond among fishermen. This thought was brought home to me as I discussed the preparation of illustrations for *Grandpa Trout* with Mitch Smith. After reviewing the first draft of *Grandpa Trout*, Mitch observed that this is not really a book about trout fishing; rather, it's a book about living, with fishing as the backdrop for telling the story.

Grandpa Trout is my grandfather's second book. His first book, *Rhymes of a Common Man*, was published in 1955. Grandpa intended to complete and publish a second book in his early retirement years. In one of the tragedies of life, this robust man who could strike out through the woods with the energy of a country boy; who had first hiked to forest streams in rural Quebec; and who had earned his living as a delivery man for the J.L. Hudson Company in Detroit, was struck ill shortly after his retirement and was not to visit his forest haunts again.

The second book languished as an incomplete project. My dad had drafts of the material typed so that the family would have a record of Grandpa's work. During the years since his death, publication of a second book remained on my mind as an obligation of tribute, love, and thanksgiving for all my grandfather had taught me and the example he set for us to live by. As a result of the sustained support of my father, Lloyd, and my uncle, Harold, *Grandpa Trout* is now alive and swimming through the rivers of thoughts and feelings of its many readers.

What you are about to read is a scrapbook of memories and stories. For the most part, the specific places described in the book are real places in Michigan, many of which I visited at my grandfather's side. I have visited the pool where the character, Grandpa Trout, was first spotted many years ago; hiked the logging trails; fished the beaver dam; and enjoyed the warmth and comraderie of hours spent around the evening campfire. I have always been fond of my grandfather's writing because it speaks to me about what's important in life and guides my thinking about what I aspire to be and how I want to live.

Grandpa hoped that, as others read his poems and stories, they would feel that special sense of recognition when common experiences are shared. Whether you enjoy these poems as you sit by a warm fireside in the winter and plan your own next trip out-of-doors, or reminisce about your own past adventures, I hope you find the excitement, insight, and mirth contained in *Grandpa Trout* to be to your liking.

I most often think of Grandpa and his poetry when I don my gear and once again prepare for a session on the trout stream. When I can, I visit one of his favorite campsites on the Manistee River. It's on a bend in the river at a place we call "the hill." It's a tremendous spot from which you can see a long stretch of river both upstream and down. The water is excellent wading depth, and the several log jams within sight create ideal trout water. As you climb down the steep bank you literally leave the everyday world behind and enter an intoxicating world of quiet, natural sounds that is a tonic for all who take the world and the material things of life a bit too seriously. I am reminded again why Grandpa loved it here. In this serene setting he was renewed, as am I. I also come here because in a deep pool off a wing dam, a little way downstream from here, I found my own "Grandpa Trout."

I sincerely hope you enjoy your visit to the world of *Grandpa Trout*.

Best Regards,

Mark Edward Jones
Publisher

Acknowledgements

In any project such as this there are many individuals who make a significant contribution. It is particularly appropriate that I acknowledge the contribution of the following few and sincerely thank them for their support and assistance in making *Grandpa Trout* a reality.

Jim Annis is an artist of considerable reputation in the areas of nature and historical art. He has created several works for the Chicago Historical Society and has received numerous awards. Jim's painting, used on the cover, is but one of his many trout and nature related works. His talent added greatly to the final look of the book. Jim makes his home and has a studio in Charlevoix, Michigan.

Roger Circle, Jr. created the portrait used in the dedication. Roger's Prophet Rock Studio in West Lafayette, Indiana creates portraits of honor for a wide range of business and community organizations. We are pleased to have reproduced his work in this book.

George Disborough produced several illustrations used in the book. His gracious widow, Janet, made them available to me, and I am grateful to be able to include his work in *Grandpa Trout*. George was an ardent angler and conservationist who is held in high regard by his fellow fishermen in the Kalamazoo, Michigan area.

Gwen Frostic also produced several illustrations. Gwen has written and illustrated 14 books and innumerable designs with a touch that is recognized around the world. She lives in Benzonia, Michigan and maintains her studio in a 285-acre wildlife sanctuary which serves as her creative library.

Tom Johns is the President of Desktop Technologies, Inc. in Ann Arbor, Michigan. From its inception, Tom has been a vigorous and patient supporter of *Grandpa Trout*. His company provided much needed assistance to translate a very rough document into the finished book for printing. For his sustained support, I am most grateful.

Tom Krol is President of Graphic Communications in Kalamazoo, Michigan. Tom designed the dust cover, helped identify sources for illustrations, and prepared some illustrations for publication. He is an avid trout fisherman and long-time member of the local chapter of Trout Unlimited.

Mitch Smith is Art Director for the Michigan United Conservation Clubs, located in Lansing, Michigan. Mitch prepared the majority of the illustrations for *Grandpa Trout*. His work is regularly displayed in MUCC publications, as well as in outdoor art exhibitions. His insight, creativity, and skillful interpretation of the poetry are greatly appreciated.

Jonathan Wright provided several illustrations for the book. Jonathan is a freelance illustrator residing in Ann Arbor, Michigan.

Last, but in no way least, I want to thank **Elizabeth M. Polmear** for her unflagging support during the project. Elizabeth was the chief editor and arbiter of style questions. She also performed the tedious work of preparing the final manuscript for printing; work that was so necessary to the book's quality, but not within my range of skills. Her work has my heartfelt appreciation. Without her unselfish efforts, this long overdue project would have taken considerably longer to complete.

There's Somethin' About Fishin'

There's Somethin' About Fishin'

Here is a poem I would like to dedicate to that great brotherhood of fishermen the world over, and that unexplainable something that tends to place all men who indulge in this wonderful pastime as fellows meeting on a common level.

It's a fascinating world, far removed from the rat race of everyday living, where hatreds and jealousies are a forgotten thing. What care you whether that fellow on the other side of the stream or in that other boat trolling around a placid lake be pauper, president or king?

In this mystic world he is simply another fisherman endeavoring to ferret out the answer to those same problems which confront you, such as the weather, or which is the most tempting fly or lure to use at this particular time.

With ever a cheerful word of greeting for that fellow on the other side of the stream as you pause to chat and perhaps exchange bits of useful information, who he is or what he is matters not. Suffice to say he's just a brother fisherman.

There's Somethin' About Fishin'

There's just somethin' about fishin',
Which a fellow can't define,
Just a certain mystic somethin',
About that world of rod and line.
Yes, there's somethin' about fishin',
Which brings out the best in men,
As it tends to make his actions,
Coincide with Godly plan.

There's somethin' about the stillness,
Which enshrouds each lake and stream,
And those friendly campfire sessions,
Where they reminisce and dream.
There's somethin' about the freshness,
Where the pine and maples grow,
The singing of the winding brook,
As its waters ebb and flow.

There's somethin' about the rainbow,
As it rises to the fly,
And the beauties of the sunset,
As it colors the western sky.
There's somethin' about the splendor,
Of the songbird's trilling call,
In that rustic world of nature,
And the grandeur of it all.

There's somethin' about the newness,
As another day has birth,
Which reminds us of God's caution,
When He mentioned, "Peace on earth."
Yes, there's somethin' about fishin',
Which brings out the best in man,
And tends to make us brothers,
All across this worldly span.

A Fisherman

"Now, just what is a fisherman?"
I asked of a friend one day,
As the old sage puffed his pipe,
In a quiet, reflective way.
He then studied me a moment,
With a twinkle in his eye,
"Good fishermen are many things,"
I heard as he made reply.

"He must be an expert driver,
With knowledge to pack a load,
Not only for the highway,
But that rugged backwoods road.
He, too, must be a boatsman,
With both oars and motors, too,
And under all conditions,
Know exactly what to do.

"He must be a weather prophet,
Able to glance up at the sky,
And predict tomorrow's weather,
With logical reasons why.
An expert, too, at reading maps,
For as difficult as it seems,
Find those many roads and trails,
To those remote lakes and streams.

"He, too, must be a patient man,
And as hours roll slowly by,
Change those lures many times,
To locate that wanted fly.
He, too, must be an engineer,
And, in just a moment, plan,
How to reach the deepest spot,
On a marshy beaver dam.

"He then must be a strategist,
And when things begin to stall,
Listen to a dozen plans,
And quickly analyze them all.
A diplomat and optimist,
And shrewd prevaricator,
A salesman tells a rosy yarn,
But the angler's must be greater.

"He should have a panther's stealth,
With a knack to disappear,
Or those trout, beyond a doubt,
Will be gone as he draws near.
He, too, must be an expert chef,
And on most primitive things,
Prepare both food and beverage,
Fit to set before the kings.

"Have the know-how of a seamstress,
With her ability to tie,
Those fine invisible leaders,
To the tiniest of flies.
He should have a doctor's knowledge,
Of all fractures, cuts and sprains,
And able to administer,
To all types of aches and pains.

"Have the stealth of an Indian,
To follow those woodland trails,
And an expert with a compass,
If in this master craft he fails.
He should be very tolerant,
With the pessimistic man,
To ferret out the good points,
Of what seems a worthless plan.

"He should be an entertainer,
And by the campfire's glowing light,
Have tales to tell in such a way,
To bring his fellowmen delight.
He should be a philosopher,
Who can expertly theorize,
Why certain fish, on certain days,
Take those certain kinds of flies.

"Have the knowledge of a lawyer,
And know all the answers, too,
As to why he should go fishing,
When there's work at home to do.
He, too, must be a sinner,
For is it not the Sabbath Day,
When those lunkers seem to rise the best,
Just to tempt good men away?

"Yes, he's a man of many traits,
From a sleuth to an artisan,
Roll all these fellows into one,
And you have a fisherman."

Heralds of Spring

There's snow in the treetops,
This first day of spring,
The robins are here,
But strange, they don't sing.
Seem rather confused,
As they flutter around,
And can't understand,
Why there's snow on the ground.

Were they mistaken,
As they flew ever north,
And followed the pattern,
Of God's given course?
They're seeking the sun,
But find only snow,
Seems Old Man Winter,
Is reluctant to go.

So rise to your rostrums,
In treetops and sing,
For you are God's heralds,
To welcome the spring.
Sing out your praises,
From red breasts that glisten,
And tree buds around you,
Will open to listen.

And beautiful leaves,
That have slumbered through cold,
Will emerge in their glory,
Of green, red and gold.
The sun in the heavens,
Will come peeping through,
To add God's warm welcome,
Of springtime to you.

Welcome those songbirds,
Which have followed you here,
Blend with them your voices,
That all mortals may hear.
Old Man Winter is leaving,
He's obeying your voice,
Stealing gently away–
He has no other choice.

So raise up your voices,
In symphonic splendor,
Hail to the trees,
To the flower buds tender.
Hail to the blossoms,
That begin to appear,
Your mission has ended,
And springtime is here.

A Perfect Day

Just to follow that trail in springtime,
To a beautiful winding stream,
A long winter's planning behind me,
As a page from a wonderful dream.
The forest about me awakened,
By the touch of God's wondrous hand,
A new gown adorns Mother Nature,
A gown only He could have planned.

It seems that as each step is taken,
And her quaint, rustic beauty unfolds,
The delicate tint of the blossoms,
In their settings of green, red and gold.
Wending my way to that crystal stream,
Through a vale of splendor and glory,
Like ending a beautiful prelude,
Beginning a wonderful story.

The sunrise cresting yon distant hill,
With the trill of the songbirds on high,
The mirrored breast of the silver stream,
Ever majestically gliding by.
Under and over a moss-cloaked log,
That would dare to dispute its flowing,
Gracefully circles a glistening rock,
Unhampered, uncaring, unknowing.

Flowing softly beneath those elders,
Overhanging with outstretching arms,
Endeavoring to capture your beauty,
And ensnare all your wonderful charms.
I watch you pause at a darkened pool,
And so peacefully there you're at rest,
As a beautiful goddess sleeping,
To replenish your vigor and zest.

My heart's drinking deep of enchantment,
My soul sheds all worry and care,
As I watch the arc of a rainbow,
While it rises and turns through the air.
Soft is the drone of the honeybee,
As I see her gracefully sway,
There's an old frog staring up at me,
In a sad and doleful sort of way.

While I assemble my rod and reel,
And just ponder those hours to come,
Tonight I'll thank a glorious God,
When this beautiful day is done.

Let's Go Fishin'

Here is a poem which I think belongs where it was conceived – by the fireside on a snowy winter's evening. It is a peaceful spot where an angler may spend his leisure hours, reminiscing of those heartwarming experiences of the season just gone by.

Perhaps you are remembering the exciting tussle with that fine smallmouth which had darted from a favorite weedbed in its effort to retrieve a well-placed lure. Whether successful in landing him or not, the memories of that lunker, leaping from the surface in his effort to dislodge that pesky plug, live on and on.

And there was that time on the Betsy River when you tangled with that beautiful brook that must have gone two pounds or better. Yes, it was the one that got away, but left you a thrilling memory which will return time and time again. The time and place are sealed in your heart, as you patiently await another season. You feel certain that fish in the same pool await your return, ready to resume the battle.

Here by the fireside a fellow seems to thumb through volumes of thrilling experiences, and dream of those wonderful hours which lay ahead, carefully noting the names and places of those lakes and streams of yesterday.

And it was here by the fireside that I felt inspired to write one of my favorite poems, "Let's Go Fishin'." In it I have endeavored to depict a stream which the great majority of trout men may vision in those cherished dreams, with pools and eddies where beautiful trout are laying in wait for that favorite fly.

Let's Go Fishin'

Come, let's go fishin', stranger,
To a favored spot of mine,
Where a lazy stream meanders,
Through a world of birch and pine.
Come, share with me those glories,
Which enhance its length and span,
All those gems of Mother Nature,
Set in a great and Godly plan.

We'll hike those winding, rustic trails,
Where its waters ebb and flow,
As we stalk the rising rainbow,
In the greatest sport I know.
I'll show you pools and riffles,
Where I think the big ones lay,
As we probe that age-old problem,
Of their pleasure for today.

We might try a midge or mayfly,
With a goodly chance to score,
Or a host of other patterns,
Which they may be waiting for.
There were times I found the answer,
But discovered to my sorrow,
The fly that makes them stir today,
They will just ignore tomorrow.

But there's heaps of fun in tryin',
To create that thrilling rise,
And a heap of satisfaction,
When you creel a fair-sized prize.
With a peacefulness about you,
Which your soul can fairly feel,
In a world of unspoiled beauty,
Which keeps repeating, "God is real."

Then as those tranquil hours,
Slowly fade into the night,
There's those hours of reminiscing,
In the campfire's glowing light.
With thrilling tales of trophies,
Which were taken yesterday,
And those frustrating stories,
Of the ones that got away.

With a mug or two of coffee,
Served in friendly sportsman's style,
A round or two of favored brew,
Which is bound to bring a smile.
I believe I called you stranger,
Then your indulgence I implore,
For beyond those peaceful hours,
We should be friends forevermore.

A Session on a Trout Stream

That session on a trout stream,
   When the evening's drawing nigh,
And those iridescent colors,
   Grace the sunset in the sky.
While those cooling evening zephyrs,
   Stir the murmur of the pine,
Just watching in the twilight,
   For that "Welcome Anglers" sign.

Scanning those pools and eddies,
   Perhaps a magic ring or rise,
In that peaceful hour of sunset,
   Lost in nature's paradise.
Far from all cares and troubles,
   So much like a beautiful dream,
That peaceful hour of waiting,
   In that session on the stream.

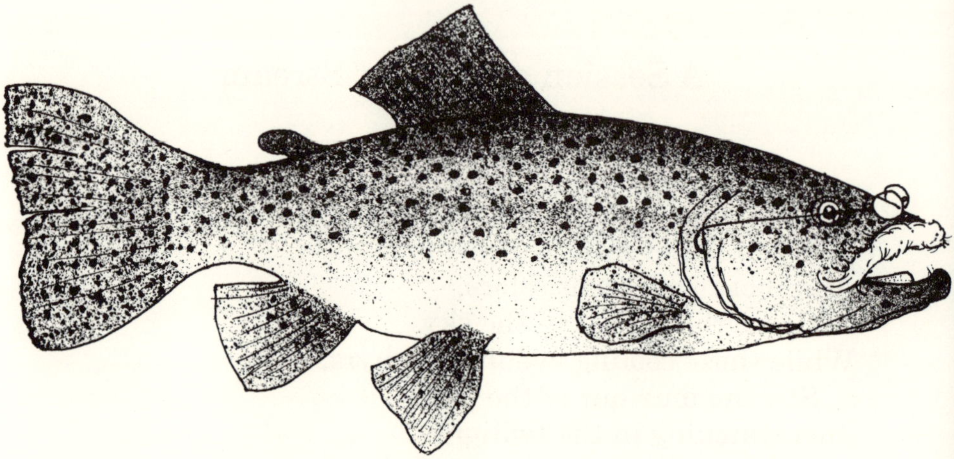

Grandpa Trout

'Twas a warm day in June 1947, when I not only received the inspiration to write the poem "Grandpa Trout," but actually experienced several frustrating hours endeavoring to outsmart this cagey old trout. They were hours spent delving into a lifetime of angling lore, trying to ferret out some solution to entice this fine specimen to strike.

At this particular time my brother-in-law, Ralph Galbreath, and I had decided to spend a week fishing one of our favorite trout streams, the good old North Branch. It was actually the north branch of the Manistee River, one of Michigan's noted trout streams. I mention it as one of our favorite streams because, in those days, we could always depend on taking our limit of trout from its waters.

I recall times when we had traveled much greater distances, even into the upper peninsula of Michigan, where we spent weeks along many fine streams in that area. However, when perhaps due to weather or other conditions not conducive to good trout fishing, we would decide to strike camp a day or so early in order to spend those extra hours on the North Branch. Usually we would have a mess of trout to take home, as it was very seldom that it failed us. Many times I heard Ralph remark, "We can always depend on the North Branch."

But please remember that was many years ago. I have fished those treasured waters a number of times since, with only mediocre success. Like many other streams in that area, it appears to be another victim of progress and changing times. In fact, on my most recent visit to this stream, I discovered that a large section had been fenced off and posted. Personally, I do not believe there could be anything in a wilderness area quite as ugly as a fence. I suppose I'll have to try and forget all those wonderful hours I've spent hiking along its trails, and the rise of those fine trout, and add them to my collection of memories.

On that last visit, after several hours of fishing its pools and eddies along an unposted area, my score totaled just two trout. They were slightly above legal size, at a time when the stream conditions appeared to be ideal. But then, who can tell about such things with any degree of certainty?

Upon returning to my car that day, I met another fellow who had been fishing downstream in the posted area. After several hours of fishing, he had only taken three trout, the largest being about twelve inches. So, here again, rather mediocre success.

We had quite a chat. It seems he had been fishing this stream over a period of twenty years. He claimed that as long as a fellow remained in the stream there was nothing anyone could do about it, whether it was posted or not. As far as he was concerned that fence meant absolutely nothing for fishing. Frankly, I do not profess to know the answer to this, as it is probably a legal question. No doubt I shall make further trips to this beautiful stream, if only to revive some of those cherished memories.

But let's get back to that week in 1947. We had arrived at the stream and set up camp in the wee hours of Sunday morning. We managed to locate beneath a couple of shade trees, a short distance from the stream.

From this location we were in a position to fish a very productive stretch of water. The trout upstream from this point ran smaller. A fellow might take three or four trout before taking one of legal size.

Ralph really enjoyed this type of fishing, as it provided plenty of action. By following a trail downstream to a spot known as the bridge, then fishing downstream from that point, a fellow would not get near as much action, but the trout ran larger and it was seldom that a trout was taken under legal size.

After setting up camp and enjoying a light lunch, we decided to hit the sack and get some needed rest. We also decided to forego any fishing on Sunday as we figured there would be other fishermen on the stream. After all, we had the entire week ahead of us, so why compete with other fishermen for that undisturbed water? So we just took things easy, worked on our tackle, and rested.

On Monday morning I crawled out of the sack with the first streaks of dawn and prepared breakfast. Shortly after sunrise, we were on our way. As was usually the case, Ralph decided that he would fish upstream, while I hiked down to the bridge and began fishing at that point. I soon discovered that the fishing on this day was not going to be very good. The sun came up bright and very warm and not at all conducive to good trout fishing. I believe on days such as this, the trout just seem to lay in the deepest water and become rather dormant. It takes a pretty attractive fly to bring them to the surface.

I made my way slowly downstream, pausing to fish those better pools which I knew so well. Then about 11 a.m., wet with perspiration from that long hike in my waders, I decided to head back to camp. As far as fishing was concerned, I had fared fairly well under the circumstances. I had managed to creel four trout, the largest being about eleven inches. All were taken on wet flies.

I had intended to fish down as far as the beaver dams, but with the day being so warm and the inner man prodding me to return to camp for lunch, I began to retrace my steps, pausing only long enough to fish some of the better pools on the way back. In so doing I managed to creel two more trout about nine inches. I'll admit I felt a little proud of this limited success on our first day.

I finally arrived at the spot known as the bridge. Actually it now consisted of two large logs spanning the stream. During the lumbering days a small gauge railway for hauling timber had crossed the stream at this point in order to haul out timber. As the trail was much easier to follow on the far side of the stream, I usually made a practice of crossing the stream here.

Making my way back across these logs, I happened to glance down into a deep hole below. I was amazed to see one of the largest trout I had ever seen in that stream. Its head was protruding from one side of a good-sized submerged log and I could make out its tail slowly moving on the other. I must have frozen there, spellbound, admiring this fine trout.

I slowly backed up along the log toward the bank I had just left, endeavoring to make as little commotion as possible in order not to alarm this beautiful trout. I then very cautiously made my way to a spot a short distance above the pool where I would be practically concealed by a clump of elders. I considered this to be an ideal spot where I would be in a position to see and not be seen.

For almost two hours I patiently changed to many patterns and sizes of flies, while making short casts over his lair. Several times I was thrilled to see him dart toward the surface as a fly to his liking floated into his line of vision, but ever refusing to actually strike. In the process of doing this, I believe I used practically every fly in my kit, both wets and dries. The best action I received on a wet fly was the Strawman Nymph, as he made several passes at this, but refused to actually take it. I had never experienced a more frustrating session.

I finally switched to live bait, but with the same result. With night crawlers, his approach was real slow. He'd come out to examine the bait and then just as slowly back up to his original position beneath the log. I sat down trying to decide just what to try next. I hoped leaving the water undisturbed for a time might do the trick. But after another frustrating session with flies, without the hint of a strike, I laid down my rod in disgust.

I sat there bemoaning my failure and trying to formulate some new plan of action when a fair-sized grasshopper within arm's reach attracted my attention. I very carefully took off my hat and placed it over the grasshopper. I tied on a #4 hook and strung the grasshopper to it. Casting it above the pool I allowed it to drift with the current.

Upon its arrival at the spot above that submerged log came the strike which I had so patiently awaited. There was a splash and my line shot downward, but lo and behold! when I set my hook I discovered I had hooked into a small trout. At the same moment I caught a glimpse of my prize trout darting upstream, probably startled by the sudden action. Thus ended my frustrating session of endeavoring to outwit the granddaddy of them all.

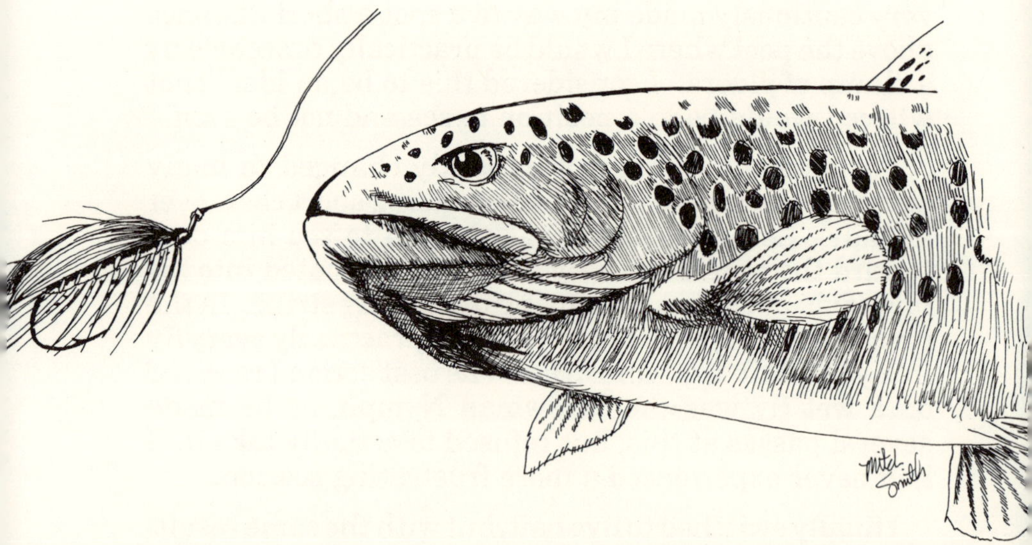

I reluctantly packed up my gear and made my way back to camp. My soul was filled with both frustration and disgust for failing to take that fine prize. Had I been successful, I certainly would have had that fine trout mounted and displayed in my den. I suppose it just wasn't my day. But to partially offset this feeling of utter frustration was a feeling of admiration for this fine trout. I consoled myself with the thought that he must have lived in that stream quite a number of years to attain such a size and, in the process, had outwitted many other fishermen much better than I.

During the following years, on numerous trips to this fine stream, it seems I was always possessed with the idea that big old trout was just laying in the same spot, waiting to resume our game of wits. Whenever I approached that pool, it was always with the utmost caution. Yes, I have found myself practically holding my breath as I paused to study its waters. Perhaps in the interim another fisherman has enjoyed the great thrill of taking this fine trout, but I cannot envision anything such as this happening. I truly believe that cagey old trout will pass on, but then due to old age.

At least it gave me the idea for the following poem, which for obvious reasons I have titled "Grandpa Trout."

Grandpa Trout

Oh, what a trout was Grandpa Trout,
Truly a speckled beauty,
So great in length and great in strength,
And as proud as he was snooty.
In his river home he lived alone,
'Neath the shade of the elder trees,
His darkened pool ran deep and cool,
And he lived a life of ease.

With logs and stumps and bushy clumps,
Settings which he took pride in,
And with danger near he had no fear,
With all those spots to hide in.
As he dozed one day in a lazy way,
When along came Shorty Trout,
Who stopped to stare at Grandpa there,
And his eyes were popping out.

He cried, "Oh dear, I dream, I fear,
Surely my eyes deceive me,
You're the greatest trout, beyond a doubt,
In all this stream, believe me."
Old Grandpa grins and moves his fins,
For a vain old trout was he,
With a surge of pride, he then replied,
"I'm just as real as real can be.

"But, lad, come here and lend an ear,
And my secrets I'll reveal,
How to thwart the plan of the monster man,
And to keep out of his creel.
Most every day he'll come this way,
With his fine and fancy gear,
And make his tries with baits and flies,
To entice me out of here.

"Beware of worms that writhe and squirm,
To escape that vicious hook,
You'll see spinners, too, which beckon you,
To dash out and take a look.
They'll use grubs and sprites and hellgrammites,
So luscious and inviting,
Many have hit at these tasty bits,
And many have left here fighting.

"You will see fine flies in every size,
To irritate and raise you,
At times they'll match the natural hatch,
And their realness will amaze you.
For a longer life, take my advice,
Be not a careless feeder,
Just train your eye to spot the fly,
That's on the telltale leader.

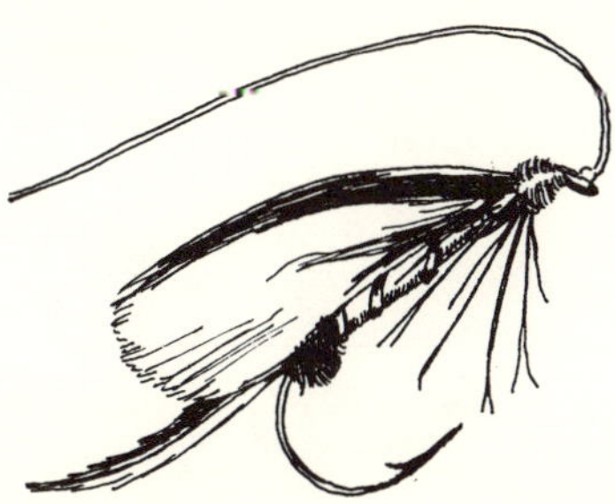

"Take heed, my boy, and play it coy,
And never let them hook you,
For if you do, I'm telling you,
They'll carve you up and cook you.
Be on your toes, as the saying goes,
And perhaps some day you'll be,
As great in length and great in strength,
And as beautiful as me.

"Now I'll say good day, be on your way,
For it's time that you departed,
I've work to do and you have, too,
For a new fly hatch has started."

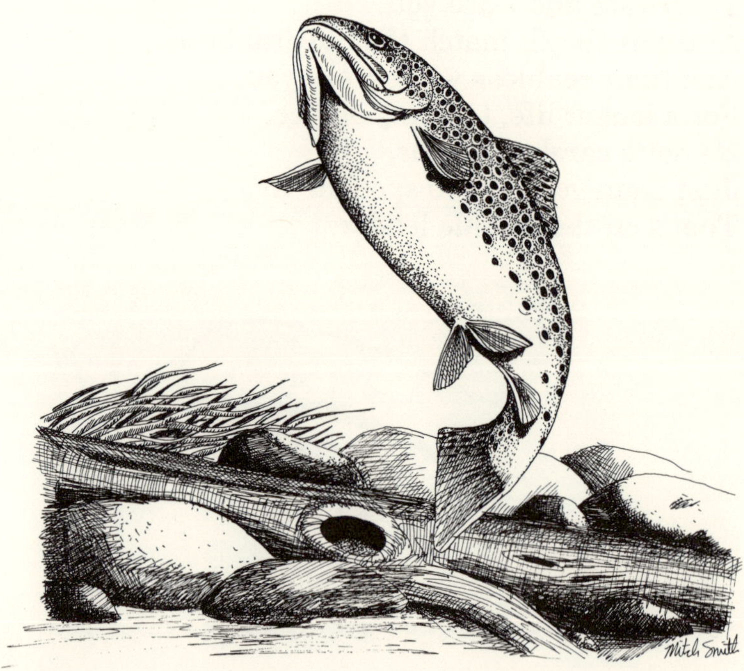

An Angler's Problems

The angler has his problems,
And I may add they are many,
So please don't classify him,
As a fellow without any.
There's the problem of a campsite,
When the old sun shines on high,
Of locating friendly shade trees,
Where the stream goes flowing by.

There's the problem of arising,
When a peaceful world says, "Sleep,"
For an early morning rendezvous,
With those game fish he must keep.
There's the problem, too, of breakfast,
As a poser he must plan,
Whether it be rolls and coffee,
Or some good old cakes and ham.

There's the problem, too, when fishing,
As it's difficult to tell,
If those trout will strike a Coachman,
Or a Parmachenie Belle.
With that ever-present problem,
Of which sizes to be using,
For they're very temperamental,
And make things quite confusing.

There's the problem, too, of weather,
At times wild, undisciplined,
And the utter frustration,
As you cast into the wind.
You watch a beauty leap and swirl,
In that darkened pool ahead,
As the placement you had hoped for,
Flutters at your feet instead.

There's those deer flies and mosquitoes,
With drone so agonizing,
Which seem to reach their greatest form,
When trout are really rising.
There's the problem of retrieving,
When a fine specimen has struck,
So alone with a landing net,
And a prayer to Lady Luck.

There's the problem of a campfire,
Where fond memories we redeem,
Will it display that friendly glow,
Or is the wood too green?
Yes, the angler has his problems,
Too numerous to mention,
I have but named a selected few,
To call to your attention.

There's the problem of the weather,
Of the campsite, and the stream,
The problem of that wanted fly,
Which may crown a cherished dream.
Down through the ages, man and boy,
Seems never could resolve 'em,
But oh I pray, a gracious God,
Allot me time to solve 'em.

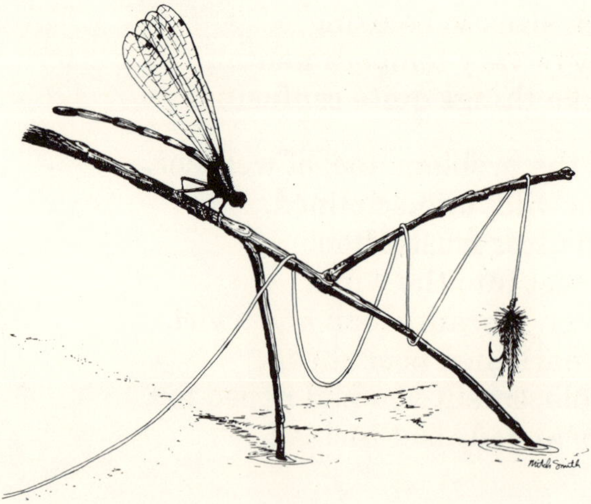

A New Stream

I paused there in the woodlands,
As I sought to find a stream,
Which bore a friend's description,
"'Tis truly an angler's dream."
My feelings were uneasy,
Of becoming lost that day,
As I blazed a mental picture,
Of some landmarks o'er the way.

Those endless vines and blossoms,
Obscuring the woodland trail,
In that rustic world of sameness,
I could not afford to fail.
'Twas then I heard its whisper,
Blended with the rustling leaves,
Much like a muted symphony,
From a world of memories.

A surge of warmth and comfort,
As my cares were swept away,
My faltering footsteps quickened,
And my heart felt light and gay.
Then closer, ever closer,
As its voice is raised in song,
Much like a hand of greeting,
Reaching out to guide me on.

Now I see its smile of welcome,
As it glistens through the trees,
Even much more beautiful,
Than those in my reveries.
I just pause in admiration,
As it goes flowing on its way,
Seems every care I've ever known,
Is remote and far away.

See the rise now of a rainbow,
As it takes an errant fly,
The thrill now of a ripple,
By that upturned tree nearby.
This symphonic natural beauty,
Only God's hand could impart,
A replica of memory,
Is etched forever in my heart.

Please lead me through your paradise,
As an old and trusted friend,
May these days go on forever,
Like your waters without end.

What Price Fishing

"Say, have you ever tried to figure,"
A fellow asked of me one day,
"What a fortune those game fish cost you,
And the money you're forced to pay?
Here, allow me to take your pencil,
As I try to figure the cost,
I'll add up all the essential things,
Plus your effort and labor lost.

fluttering caddis

"The figure no doubt will amaze you,
When you see the sum that you pay,
That's the reason why I buy my fish,
From the market across the way."
"You probably are right, my friend,
And no doubt your figures are true,
But while you're jotting down those items,
Allow me to add just a few.

"A camp by a lake in the evening,
With a pale moon shining on high,
Its beautiful waters reflecting,
Those eons of stars in the sky.
Where you hear the call of a night bird,
That's perched in a tree o'er the way,
With yesterday's sorrows forgotten,
And tomorrow a happier day.

"Then add all those beautiful pine trees,
All standing so tall and so straight,
I fear it's something your pencil, sir,
Can never fully evaluate.
Then let's picture the natural beauty,
Where a quaint forest trail winds through,
Tell me, just what is such splendor worth, sir,
To a practical man such as you?

"And then add the beautiful sunset,
Glorifying the western sky,
When you can almost hear God saying,
'Another wonderful night is nigh.'
Yes, it's there to cheer the heart of man,
Bring peace to his soul and enthuse,
Now, to put this all down on paper,
Tell me, what figures would you use?

"There's the rising of the trout at dawn,
And the honeybee's sweet drone,
A nest above where the branches fork,
And a songbird has made its home.
Or casting a bait near the weedbeds,
From a boat anchored there off shore,
You feel there's a lunker just waiting,
As you cast out that plug once more.

"And then comes the strike you expected,
You're a-thrill to the stirring sight,
As the critter leaps from the water,
And seems to stand on his tail to fight.
It's really the thrill of a lifetime,
When these fighters go into their act,
So, what with your pencil and paper,
Could you possibly add or subtract?

"Or maybe the story is different,
Perhaps there's not even a bite,
You still have that forest about you,
And a warm glowing campfire at night.
With the whispering of the pine trees,
The gay, merry song of the stream,
Away from the noise of the city,
While breathing air, pure and clean.

"So, I trust you will understand, sir,
All these beautiful things which I feel,
The angler's world offers so much more,
Than the heft of a weighted creel."

The Ardent Fisherman

Now Chuck was quite a fisherman,
An ardent sportsman, through and through,
And when fishing season opened,
There was just naught else he would do.
Throughout the months of ice and snow,
He was an average, real nice guy,
Took care of things around the house,
Without question or reason why.

But when old springtime rolled around,
He almost drove his wife berserk,
For no matter how Liz pleaded,
He just simply would not work.
Just to get his mind on painting,
Liz brought home a color chart,
And sat mooning over colors,
That were the dearest to her heart.

She said, "Honey, I like suntan,
So much better than the peach,"
Chuck replied, "That's O.K., darling,
But we can get it at the beach."
When Liz suggested cleaning up,
To make things look more becoming,
He vetoed that idea right away,
With, "You know the smelt are running."

The drawers were filled with tackle,
Her lovely drapes were full of flies,
To break dates for social functions,
Old Chuck would tell the darnedest lies.
There were crickets in the bird cage,
And hooks imbedded in the couch,
While an oft-time used expression,
Was the sharp painful cry of, "Ouch."

Then one day in the laundry room,
Where Liz had gone to wash some togs,
And the laundry tubs were swarming,
With lively hellgrammites and frogs.
She dashed up the stairway screaming,
I had to duck to let her pass,
While Chuck stood close by explaining,
"Why, they're the greatest bait for bass."

Another day, when I dropped in,
They seemed to be on friendly terms,
'Til Liz opened up the ice box,
And found a mess of worms.
She stood there almost petrified,
With Chuck trying hard to please,
By gathering up the crawlers,
From the butter, eggs and cheese.

But the worst of all Chuck told me,
Was when Liz just about dropped dead,
As a big old snapping turtle,
Crawled out from underneath her bed.
"Boy, the names that night she called me,
A crazy imbecile, and droop,
And it seemed to make no difference,
That I was saving it for soup."

I decided to stop callin',
So rugged was their marital course,
For the way that things were going,
They'd be heading for divorce.
Then I met Liz some time later,
And was amazed she seemed so gay,
As she extended me her hand,
In such a pleasant sort of way.

She said, "Now we're oh so happy,
And life is so much like a song."
I asked her if she'd trained the lug?
She replied, "Oh, no, I go along."

The Enchanted Stream

I believe "The Enchanted Stream" was among the first poems I wrote. The inspiration for this poem was provided by an actual experience while fishing the Little Two Hearted River in upper Michigan.

On this occasion my brother-in-law, Ralph Galbreath, and I had made camp on the river a short distance above the Shamrock Bridge, where we found the fishing to be slightly above average. But those distant fields ever appear to be greener, and there is the angler's dream of big old lunkers waiting patiently for that careless fly. Yes, somewhere, away from the beaten track, where the stream meanders aimlessly through a vast wilderness, there is a place where speckled beauties merely die of old age.

With all this in mind, on the third day of our trip we drove upstream along an old logging road. After several miles it seemed to fade into a world of trees and underbrush. Here we parked the car and listened to the voice of the stream as it wended its way over logs and rocks which dared to stem its progress.

With that ever-present feeling of anticipation which it seems the good Lord reserves for those brothers of the angle, we assembled our gear, checked on the time, and discussed our plan of action. Ralph elected to fish upstream, while I fished that area below our starting point.

We planned on returning to the car at 11 a.m. This would allow us about three hours of fishing. With our dreams of lunker trout rising to every cast, the time allotted seemed more than adequate.

But as best laid plans often go awry, I discovered that this area was no better than the section down below where our camp was located. During the first hour I had managed to creel two brooks about ten inches in length. The stream was very winding, with underbrush making progress rather difficult. On many occasions I was obliged to merely float the fly ahead of me with the current. I would have probably fared much better with live bait, but unfortunately I hadn't brought any along.

I finally arrived at an excellent looking pool where the stream made a sharp turn. The water seemed to be quite deep. A slight open area provided me with room to cast. After casting over different sections of this pool without success, I was rewarded with a beautiful strike and creeled a fourteen incher. With this my sagging spirits again skyrocketed. I spent thirty or forty minutes casting several patterns and sizes over this pool and managed to take two more trout, averaging about ten inches, before moving on. During the following hour I caught two more brooks making a total of seven.

It was now 10 a.m. and, deciding to allow myself an hour in which to return to the car, I packed up and headed back. By this time the sun was high in the heavens and hiking was very difficult. Soaked with perspiration, I decided to head away from the stream toward the higher ground where the walking was less difficult. At the time, I believed I knew where I was going and finding the car would be no problem. Unfortunately, this was not the case. I managed to bypass the car and head into an endless wilderness beyond.

Usually being lost in the woods is a rather frightening experience. You are there alone in a strange world, uncertain which direction to follow, pausing occasionally, endeavoring to decide on some sort of bearing, whistling and calling, hoping to hear some response, but hearing nothing more than the voice of forest, the whisper of the pines, and the constant trill of the birds. Once again moving forward, you wonder whether you are traveling a circular course and try to avoid doing so, ever alert for some sort of feeder stream. In my estimation a feeder stream is a lost person's best friend, as it not only provides a cool drink, but usually guides one back to the main stream.

I had been wandering for what seemed like an eternity. I checked the time; it was almost 3 p.m. At this point I began contemplating spending the night in the woods. All in all, it can be a truly harrowing experience.

But on this particular day, although realizing I was lost, somehow I never experienced this feeling of emptiness. Perhaps after you read the accompanying poem, "The Enchanted Stream," you may understand the reason why. Being a lover of the great outdoors, I have always contended there is nothing quite as beautiful as a forest setting where a stream flows through a world of natural splendor. The stately trees, the vines and wild flowers, the trill of the birds, it seems to me this unspoiled world is part of heaven itself and truly the work of a gracious God.

Getting back to the predicament which I had so carelessly blundered into that day, I will say that the beauty all about me seemed to more than compensate for that feeling of dismay. I finally decided on a plan to keep the sun over my shoulder and sort of follow my shadow in my effort to follow a direct course. I believe the good Lord was with me, as in a short time the sparkling song of the winding stream wafted to my ears through the trees ahead. I don't believe I have ever heard anything more beautiful, my heart engulfed with a feeling of enchantment, for both its beauty and its song. I quickened my pace as it guided me back to that time worn bridge and a worried and fretful Ralph. Yes, it was both a harrowing and beautiful experience and I have endeavored to record it in the following lines of "The Enchanted Stream."

The Enchanted Stream

I lost myself in a woods one day,
And strange as it may be,
Those several hours I sought my way,
My heart felt strangely free.
I'd wandered down a forest lane,
Between the virgin pines,
Like cathedral spires against the sky,
With a thousand forest chimes.

Bluebird, thrush and robin,
Filled the air with song,
And watched me with suspicion,
As though I'd done some wrong.
So Eden-like and beautiful,
As onward there I trod,
And many times I paused to view,
This handiwork of God.

Many flowers and blossoms,
That I found growing there,
Free and unattended,
Lent fragrance to the air.
Tall and stately birch trees,
With bark so pure and white,
Seemed to stand like beacons,
That guide you through the night.

The forest shadows dancing,
On sunbeams through the trees,
Like a ballet, so entrancing,
Swaying gracefully in the breeze.
And then I heard the singing,
Seemed almost like a dream,
The sweet and rhythmic melody,
Of a winding forest stream.

Rare symphonies from old masters,
It caused me to recall,
As it gently flowed in riffles,
Then found a waterfall.
Ebbing and a-whirling,
And then to onward rush,
At times in perfect harmony,
With the singing of the thrush.

Enchanted there, I followed,
The way the stream was flowing,
Not pausing for a second thought,
To where I might be going.
So carefree, then, and happy,
To be following along,
Just lost in all its beauty,
Enraptured by its song.

Reflecting like rare emeralds,
The virgin pines so high,
Then gently through a clearing,
The azure of the sky.
Flowing past the willows,
Through gardens of green fern,
Then back into the woodlands,
As gracefully it turned.

Its melody was blending,
With feathered friends on high,
Cedars bowing in reverence,
In praise as it went by.
Then quite unbeknowingly,
The rhapsody had ended,
For there beneath a roadway,
My singing stream had wended.

I tarried long beside the bridge,
For a long and lasting look,
To end a beautiful chapter,
In my life's memory book.

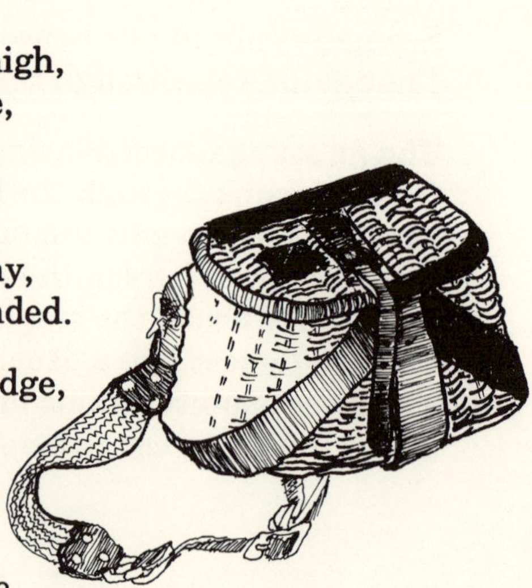

The Stranger

A stranger paused to chat one day,
As I prepared a little snack,
At a lakeside camp I'd set up,
Far away from the beaten track.
Though totally unknown to him,
We seemed to have so much to say,
As we shared a pot of coffee,
In a friendly sort of way.

We discussed the trees and flowers,
Growing along that woodland trail,
We compared the many beauties,
Nature in springtime will unveil.
Of the dams made by the beaver,
And of the chipmunks at their play,
As we shared a pot of coffee,
In a friendly sort of way.

Then we talked of homes and gardens,
Proudly talked of children, too,
Perhaps boasted just a little,
As doting dads are apt to do.
Of the colors of the sunset,
As evening ushers out the day,
As we shared a pot of coffee,
In a friendly sort of way.

We relived cherished memories,
Of trips to forest, lake and stream,
We discussed those splendid trophies,
Of which all sportsmen like to dream.
Quite omitted were the hatreds,
Which so enshroud our world today,
As we shared a pot of coffee,
In a friendly sort of way.

We never mentioned stocks or bonds,
Whether they be high or low,
For business seemed so out of place,
In that world where memories glow.
Aye, I felt a little saddened,
As I watched him depart that day,
I saw him turn and wave his hand,
In a friendly sort of way.

As the evening shadows lowered,
And many stars danced up above,
While the campfire gently sparked,
With quiet tranquility and love.
Then I thanked God for his blessings,
And the friend I'd found that day,
As we shared a pot of coffee,
In a friendly sort of way.

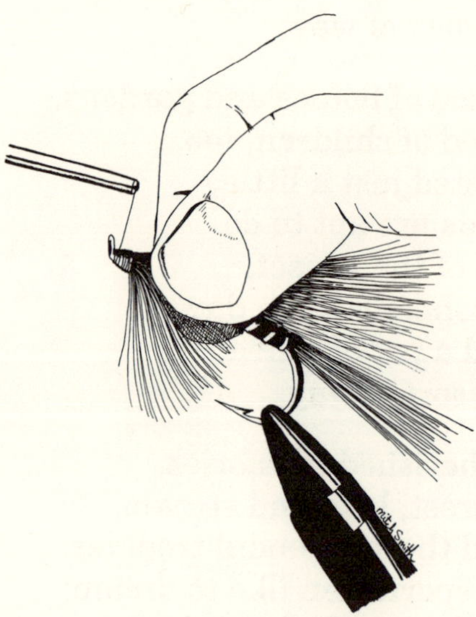

Beaver Dam

With those evening shadows falling,
Shades of night fast drawing nigh,
I paused beside that beaver dam,
To select another fly.
I'd been on the stream since daybreak,
All its wonders to explore,
Along that winding, rustic trail,
And should have turned back long before.

It was then I saw it shining,
Like a mirror through the trees,
As the flowing waters whispered,
Through a thousand arteries.
A great masterpiece of nature,
By its most skilled craftsman,
A true wonder of the woodlands,
Is the hidden beaver dam.

As I stepped slowly o'er its crest,
Of those branches intertwined,
Like entering another world,
With all realities behind.
I watched a pool below the dam,
Where those rivulets joined force,
And seemed to pause before flowing on,
Their beautiful winding course.

My attention was arrested,
By a tiny glistening frog,
And the shadow of a rainbow,
Seeking the refuge of a log.
Then I paused there contemplating,
Where to make my opening cast,
With forest shadows lengthening,
And day fleeting all too fast.

Arrested in its backward flight,
My fly line gracefully twirled,
I saw a ripple on the pool,
Where a rising rainbow swirled.
Now the pattern I had chosen,
I'm afraid I don't recall,
But the way those trout were rising,
Well, it mattered not at all.

Just the lateness of the hour,
Was my one and sole regret,
As I played those fighting beauties,
In toward my waiting net.
Then I glanced toward the pine trees,
Like gaunt shadows on the hill,
They seemed to stand like sentinels,
So tall, so straight, so still.

Dozens of tiny frogs gave voice,
To their evening serenade,
And the sun had left the heavens,
In quaint shades of gold and jade.
The beautiful forest slumbered,
As though God had whispered, "Rest,"
And gone the trilling of the birds,
They had once more sought their nest.

Michigan

Michigan

M stands for the millions
of your tall and stately pine.
I the many islands
which dot your lakes so fine.
C is for the cedars
that grace your winding streams.
H the hardwood forests
which border your ravines.
I means the Indian legends
we read about with pride.
G stands for the Great Lakes
which lie on every side.
A means the abundance
of many kinds of game.
N the natural beauty
to which you owe your fame.

That's Michigan the beautiful,
So rustic and so grand,
A masterpiece of nature,
The water wonderland.

The Water Wonderland

I have dedicated this poem to the thousands of miles of meandering streams to be found throughout the state of Michigan, to the countless hours of pleasure and joy that have been mine while hiking along their rustic trails, and to all the thrills I have experienced with the rise of their fine trout.

Until the time I wrote this poem I had more or less taken them for granted. I may never have taken the time to meditate on the subject had it not been for an interesting discussion I had with a friend of mine one Sunday morning, while we were camped on the Big Manistee River.

As I recall it was early in August 1960. My young son, Casey, and I had arrived at the river and set up camp the previous evening. Following our long drive from home, Casey had elected to forego any fishing Sunday morning and enjoy a few extra hours of sleep. But with those lunkers in mind, I was up and about at daylight, planning to get in a few hours of fishing before other fishermen put in an appearance. Following a quick cup of coffee and a sweet roll, I donned my waders and headed downstream shortly after 6 a.m. I hiked to a spot about three quarters of a mile downstream and began fishing at that point. I figured this would allow sufficient time for Casey to get those extra hours of sleep, and at the same time provide me with an undisturbed session of fishing in the early morning hours when I enjoyed it the most.

I slowly began making my way back towards camp, pausing frequently to fish the better looking pools and wing dams. I had a nice strike shortly after entering the river, but, due to over anxiety I suppose, I failed to hook him. I spent the following moments reprimanding myself because of it.

On the next strike old Lady Luck happened to be on my side and I managed to creel a nice ten inch rainbow. After that spirit raising event I had almost an hour of frustration, during which time I diligently plied numerous patterns and sizes of flies over promising looking water without a strike.

By this time I had covered almost half the distance back to camp and was beginning to feel a little dejected about my mediocre success. I considered calling it a day and hiking back to camp, but as I had just tied on a #10 Parmachenie Belle, I decided to continue a few minutes longer. I was rewarded for my decision by another strike, but again I missed, plunging me into another session of condemnation and cussing. I don't know whether this helps or not, but at least on this occasion it seemed to change my luck. By the time I arrived at camp I had creeled three more bows averaging about nine inches.

I discovered Casey was still far away in the land of nod. I had developed quite an appetite in that session on the river so I began preparing a breakfast of hot cakes and sausage plus a good old pot of coffee. With this task almost completed, I began to set the table, when I noticed another angler heading up the trail from the river.

"Hi," he greeted me as he arrived at the top of the rise. "Do you happen to be Lloyd Jones's dad?"

"That's right," I answered. "Then you must be George, who Lloyd has told me about many times. He thinks you are just about the greatest when it comes to trout fishing. Did you have any luck today?"

"I believe I got nine or ten," George replied, lifting the lid of his creel and holding up a brook that must have measured twelve inches. I realized at that moment that all those things Lloyd had told me about George's trout fishing ability were not figments of imagination.

"How long were you on the river? What fly were you using?" I asked, firing a barrage of questions.

"I started downstream, where that road approaches the stream about a mile down. That nice brook I caught on a Montana Mite. In fact I believe I got the majority of them on the same fly. I don't believe they have them in Michigan. Here let me show you one." He opened a well stocked fly box and took one out. It was brown in color, a wet fly with a well rounded body, and what appeared to be a circle of stiff hairs laying back from the neck. It was not a pretty fly by any means, but apparently it must have looked good to those trout.

"Here," George said, removing another one from the box. "Try them out on your next fishing session. They seem to do very well for me. Let me know how you make out with them, and if you wish, I can send you and Lloyd a couple of dozen the next time I am in Livingstone, Montana. By the way, Lloyd should be along shortly. He dropped me off downstream, and then drove up to the next road above your camp. He planned to fish downstream a ways and then hike back to the car, and we decided on meeting here about 11 o'clock."

"Well, that will just give us time to tie into a stack of hot cakes and sausage," I replied. "And don't say you're not hungry. You see, I just got back from a fishing session a short time ago and I'm starved. I know you must be too. Sit down and dig in."

"Well, you will not have to twist my arm," George replied. "They really look good. This is what I call really living, enjoying a fine breakfast right on the river."

And thus it was under these ideal circumstances that I became acquainted with George Block. He may not be the greatest trout fisherman in the country, but at least he is one of the finest I've ever had the pleasure of being acquainted with.

During breakfast the topic of conversation dealt mostly with Michigan and trout fishing, as this trip to Michigan was an annual event for George and his beautiful wife and daughter. By prearrangement, both Lloyd and George reserved cottages at Starvation Lake which provided swimming and boating for their families, while being within easy driving distance to the Big Manistee for trout fishing. It was an ideal setup for all concerned.

It seems that George, besides spending this week trout fishing in Michigan, also made numerous trips to many noted streams in other states to indulge in this great sport. "But," he confided, "I always enjoy this trip to Michigan the best of all." This statement coming from an expert in the art of angling lore was really something. It made me realize that the old Manistee must be a pretty fair stream after all.

Just about the time we finished breakfast, Lloyd drove in in time to join us for that second cup of coffee. I wanted to prepare another stack of cakes for him and, although I could see he was tempted, he explained that Carol would have breakfast waiting, so he had better save his appetite. He had taken five nice bows while fishing upstream, so this first session of fishing had been fairly good, with George leading the parade.

Before leaving they invited Casey and I to join them in a cookout at the lake that evening. I gratefully accepted, realizing that these cookouts are gala events and worlds of fun.

That interesting discussion I had with George provided me with plenty of food for thought, as I began to realize that through the years I had more or less taken these fine Michigan streams for granted. I began to recall all the hours I had spent fishing the many different streams throughout the state. Thus with all those fine trout streams in mind, I endeavored to pay tribute to their greatness. And what better title could I use than "The Water Wonderland?"

The Water Wonderland

As the sun shines there in the heavens,
There's sweet nectar of spring in the air,
With rainbows a-leap in the rivers,
And you're sortin' that tackle with care.
Once more you're plannin' and dreamin',
Cherished visions which just come and go,
You ponder those streams in the Catskills,
And rare spots on the old Pocono.

Those jewels of the quaint Adirondacks,
And all those wonders of Yellowstone,
If only those beautiful trout streams,
Were a little bit closer to home.
Those wonderful streams of Montana,
All these visions make you wish again,
But let's not overlook the wonders,
Of our rustic and quaint Michigan.

Though you travel this country over,
I have doubt that you ever will see,
A stream which displays more allurement,
Than our beautiful Big Manistee.
I believe God took the Au Sable,
From a nook in some heavenly glen,
And placed it here in a sea of pine,
Much like a rare and priceless gem.

If confined to but one adjective,
To describe the Jordan and the Slate,
I should be forced to add another,
For they are both beautiful and great.
And where will you find another stream,
To surpass our beautiful Pine?
Shimmering along through the woodlands,
As a jewel in a rustic shrine.

There's the Big and Little Two Hearted,
Adding so much to Michigan's name,
Ever famed for their scenic beauty,
And equally famous for their game.
We have the Sturgeon and the Pigeon,
Which bring on memories so devout,
Of cherished hikes o'er their pine-cloaked trails,
And the thrill to the rise of their trout.

The song of the Au Gres and Rifle,
Tells of beautiful rainbows at play,
Or you might try the Black or Betsy,
Where fine brookies will brighten your day.
It seems I could go on forever,
Eulogizing our beautiful streams,
So many have left a memory,
Forever flowing through my dreams.

I've no doubt there are far off places,
Equally as beautiful and grand,
But I'll pitch my tent in Michigan,
A wonderful water wonderland.

The Au Sable

Wending its way through my cherished dreams,
There's a beautiful, sparkling gem,
Its settings arranged by God alone,
Forever beckoning to all men.
You will see them in the early dawn,
And again when the sunset glows,
Casting about, for those flashing trout,
Where the quaint Au Sable flows.

Just to dip my paddle once again,
In its sparkling waters, so clear,
Let the man-made world recede and fade,
With paradise so near.
Oh to glide along its mirrored breast,
Much like the red men long ago,
And just relax in sheer content,
Where the quaint Au Sable flows.

As fair as a beautiful goddess,
Ever unspoiled by the hand of man,
Those tranquil settings unfolding,
In every nook of its length and span.
Regal pines, willows and birches,
With every beautiful thing that grows,
There graciously wait to greet you,
Where the quaint Au Sable flows.

Let me tarry beside its bridges,
In all their old and rustic splendor,
To read inscriptions patiently carved,
By those fellows who would remember.
Here is Mother Nature at her best,
To greater towering heights, she rose,
To decorate so wonderfully,
Where the quaint Au Sable flows.

A Toast To Michigan

Oh, Michigan's northland here I come,
With my winter's work and planning done;
And the old car loaded down once more,
For those carefree days you hold in store.

Along that winding road, through hill and vale,
Leading to that happy, carefree trail;
All cares and troubles left behind me,
Though they may seek, they'll never find me.

May I find fish, of every species,
The kind that tear my gear to pieces;
With flies all the finest on the list,
Which your fighting rainbows can't resist.

There's wishful thinking in this writing,
Perhaps those big ones are not biting;
But my cherished dream cannot impair,
For your natural beauty is ever there.

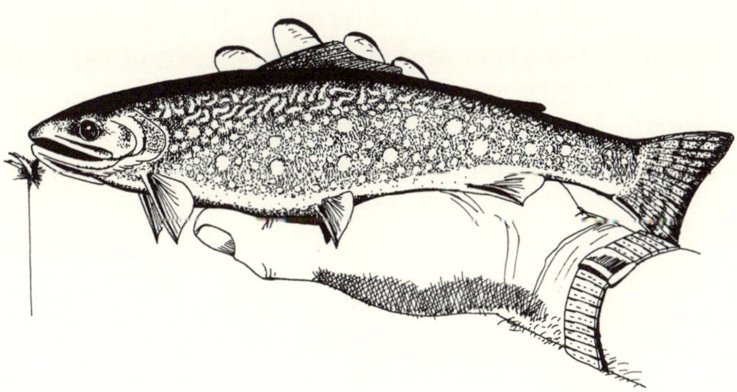

Trout Water

I received the idea for the poem, "Trout Water," in July 1955 while conversing with an elderly gentleman one evening on the porch of a convalescent home in Caro, Michigan. We sat there exchanging a few pleasantries and indulging in small talk, when the subject finally got around to trout fishing. The old fellow's eyes seemed to light up like a Christmas tree and the thought occurred to me, "Now here's a real old-time trout fisherman."

Naturally in discussions of this sort, cherished experiences are recalled, and favorite streams compared. It seems that in his younger days he had lived on the outskirts of Newberry, Michigan. I believe the stream he began describing to me must have been a section of the Little Two Hearted River. I have enjoyed the pleasure of fishing its waters on numerous occasions. I recall taking many fine trout from its waters and the forest splendor to be found along its winding course, especially that area around the Crow's Nest Bridge.

I was fascinated by that old gentleman's description of its pools and eddies, the natural beauty to be found along its banks, and those beautiful trout. It was truly a masterpiece of eloquence, and his descriptive version of this cherished stream was poetry in itself. During the weeks following our discussion, I endeavored to translate his words into poetry. Perhaps I should have titled this poem, "The Little Two Hearted," but not being certain about the name of the stream, I decided on the title of "Trout Water."

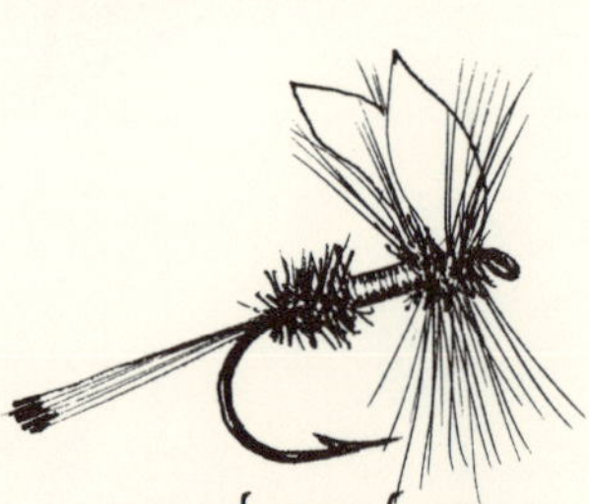

royal coachman

Trout Water

Did I hear you mention fishin'?
Why that's the best suggestion yet,
Let me take you on a trip, sir,
Which I'm sure you'll not forget.
Kindly state your pleasure, sir,
I believe you mentioned trout,
Then my tale is made to order,
Beyond the shadow of a doubt.

Let me take you to a stream, sir,
Which I fished many years ago,
And through my cherished memories,
Its waters ever ebb and flow.
I do not know its terminus,
And I'd never found its source,
But I know one beautiful stretch,
There along its winding course.

With those lurking brooks and rainbows,
To gladden the angler's eye,
Layin' there watchin' and waitin',
For that errant nymph or fly.
Yes, I'd hike in there at daybreak,
When all was peaceful-like and still,
With the old sun barely crestin',
The beauties of the distant hill.

Just the murmur of the waters,
As they went windin' on their way,
An' the trillin' of a songbird,
Beckonin' in another day.
With the old heart beatin' faster,
Sortin' flies in contemplation,
An' my fingers all a-tremble,
In pent-up anticipation.

Boy, that first hole was a dandy,
Let me describe it to you, man,
At the top end, real fast water,
And at the lower end, a dam.
Where the waters swirled in anger,
At this sudden interruption,
They seemed to pause an' sulk a bit,
Before clearing this obstruction.

Aye, that was a favored spot, sir,
For both those lovely trout and I,
An' they really wasn't fussy,
Of my selection of a fly.
At times I tossed them an Adams,
Or just a plain old Squirrel tail,
An' brother it was seldom,
That I would fish that hole and fail.

Well, that's where I'd begin, sir,
An' then start my hike upstream,
Through a panorama of beauty,
Such as you have seldom seen.
I'd pause to fish the riffles,
Or perhaps near a fallen tree,
An' where the banks were undercut,
All those spots appealed to me.

Sometimes standin' in the rapids,
With white water flashin' by,
An' in that darkened pool below,
I had managed to place a fly.
When suddenly I hear a splash,
Even above the roar an' din,
An' I know I've hooked a lunker,
As the old reel begins to spin.

I'm wonderin' how to land him,
While seekin' a better stance,
Tryin' to keep the line real taut,
An' I'm watchin' that rod tip dance.
Well, that's the trip I promised, sir,
I'd like to take you there sometime,
It would really be a tonic,
For this tired old heart of mine.

Say, we'll hike in there together,
An' when that great day is done,
I'll guarantee that stream of streams,
Another life-long friend has won.

Mackinaw Bridge

Up where those mighty girders of steel,
Much like silhouettes etched on the sky;
While below giant pillars of concrete,
Seem to slumber as waters drift by.
With the glare of countless beams of light,
Piercing the darkness across the span;
The roar of motors throughout the day,
All in tribute to efforts of man.

The miracle of the century,
And recorded as one of our greats;
Quite a tribute to engineering,
Is "Big Mac" which is spanning the straits.
Gone now are those slow moving ferries,
Gone, too, the relaxation and rest;
For here is the bridge many dreamed of,
If continuous driving is best.

You recall when leaving the ferries,
Very soon Mother Nature you'd find;
But now it seems we must drive for miles,
Ere we leave all those bright lights behind.
Ever seeking that natural beauty,
In a wonderland all sportsmen prized;
A world which is fast disappearing,
With it becoming commercialized.

Those deer will be gone from the highway,
With the flash of the bright neon sign;
As we dream of those days when we saw them,
Staring back 'neath the shade of the pine.
Aye, we'll watch as old Mother Nature,
Reluctantly gives up her land;
Stepping aside for modernization,
Ever yielding to humans' demand.

Those fine men of conservation,
Who through the years have won much acclaim;
Will gallantly stand there beside her,
But their efforts will all be in vain.
'Tis useless to fight against progress,
When that progress means riches, you know;
The law of the almighty dollar,
Means every last barrier must go.

No, the day is not too far distant,
A day all true sportsmen will rue;
An unbroken line of business spots,
From St. Ignace on up to the Soo.
When most of the wildlife has vanished,
Driven off with the coming of man;
Again we'll turn to that mighty bridge,
And detest every inch of its span.

Those men who had flocked to the Upper,
Seeking a share of its pot of gold;
Will gradually learn that fortune's hand,
Had grown heartless, and clammy, and cold.
A beautiful country, vast and still,
With naught left for the sportsman's plan;
The bridge will stand as a monument,
To the colossal error of man.

Song of the Porkies

The Porcupine Mountain area, located at the tip of upper Michigan, is perhaps one of the last sections of the great state of Michigan to retain all its natural and rugged beauty, unmarred and unspoiled through the years. I received the inspiration for the following poem after reading of quite a debate in the state capital. It seems that representatives of a large mining company were desirous of obtaining a large tract of land located in this beautiful wilderness in order to begin mining operations.

The opposition was made up of lovers of nature who were fighting to keep this rustic paradise just as God had planned it. Personally, I hope it will remain suffused in all its natural splendor and beauty until the end of time.

Song of the Porkies

I'm known as the Porcupine Mountains,
Aye, I'm one of the last frontiers,
Still refulgent in natural beauty,
Unmarred and unspoiled through the years.
In that raiment, just as God planned me,
All work of his wondrous hand,
From those breathtaking peaks above me,
To my valleys where tall pine stand.

Aye, send me those men who are rugged,
Who worship the gems I display,
Here deep in the heart of my woodlands,
And here they are welcome to stay.
Let me show them my lakes and rivers,
Unspoiled by invasion of man,
And these I shall take to my bosom,
Only these are my chosen clan.

For these are the men who protect me,
From those that would tear me apart,
Who parry the thrust of the dagger,
Ever aimed at my stalwart heart.
Those men who appreciate riches,
Far greater than money or gems,
My endless tracts of natural splendor,
Mean much more than riches to them.

There's my wonderful lakes and rivers,
My birches, my hemlock and pine,
Solace they'll find here in God's wonders,
In this great rustic world of mine.
Come, gather ye then by my campfires,
Speak of glories I offered today,
Hark now while they hack at my borders,
Drink deep of me yet while ye may.

South of the Cameron Road Bridge

The ideas for many of the poems in this book are gathered from actual experiences, perhaps an interesting conversation while sitting by the campfire on a starlit night, or an unusual experience along a meandering trout stream, or a beautiful locale where luckily I have made camp. The poem, "South of the Cameron Road Bridge," was one of the latter.

In July 1960, my youngest son, Casey, and I were enjoying a two-week vacation of trout fishing in northern Michigan. Casey had attained the age of thirteen and had developed into a pretty fair trout fisherman. He had been accompanying me on these trips since he was five years old and enjoyed every minute of them.

Fishing had been fairly good that first week and the weather was just about perfect. We had made camp on the Big Manistee River, a short distance above DeWard. This had been a thriving lumbering town during the logging days in Michigan, but as the cutting of timber ended and the lumbermen moved away, the town literally disappeared. In fact, all that remains is an old brick chimney, which has become a marker of those historic logging days in Michigan.

Being members of the Dearborn Woods and Waters Club of Dearborn, Michigan, we had arranged to spend the second week at a small lodge on the Jordan River that was owned by the club. After taking down our camp and driving to the lodge, we discovered that another member of the club had moved in with his family. They happened to be away at the time of our arrival, but we noticed a store of groceries, plus clothing, and realized that the schedule had become fouled up somewhere along the line.

As it was almost 5 p.m. and there was not much daylight left, we drove back to the Manistee River. This time we bypassed DeWard and continued on, making a right turn onto the river road beyond the Cameron Road Bridge. A short distance down this road we arrived at a beautiful campsite, and again set up camp. This happened to be one of the most beautiful spots I had ever camped in. The fishing that second week was all that could be desired. In fact, we enjoyed that week of camping so much that it gave me the idea for the poem, "South of the Cameron Road Bridge."

South of the Cameron Road Bridge

A wee bit south of the Cameron Bridge,
On the beautiful Manistee,
Lies a tract of unspoiled beauty,
Latticed in nature's artistry.
With towering pine, and glowing birch,
Spreading maples in leafy gown,
Each standing in rustic splendor,
Much like jewels in a regal crown.

And stretching o'er that forest floor,
Lies a carpet of ferns so green,
Selected by Mother Nature,
To complete this beautiful scene.
Here where the river separates,
As young lovers who sulk and pout,
Swirling apart in eddies and pools,
As havens for fighting trout.

Where the Adams and the Coachman,
Perhaps a Dun or Ginger Quill,
Cast slowly o'er its mirrored breast,
By hand and heart that's all a-thrill.
At times there may be a ripple,
As a bow takes a closer look,
But oft-times comes that treasured rise,
As he leaps to the feathered hook.

Perhaps the story is different,
Long hours with nary a rise,
Consorting with old Mother Nature,
In the heart of her paradise.
To name my favorite campsite,
I believe that my choice would be,
A wee bit south of the Cameron Bridge,
On the beautiful Manistee.

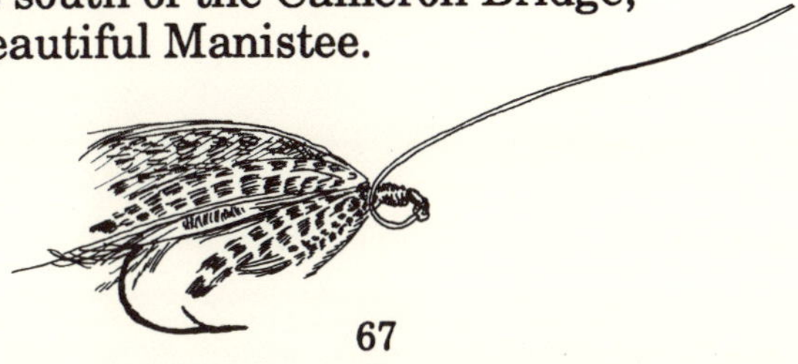

Campfire Tales

Campfire Tales

Come, join me, friend, by the campfire,
    Let us hark to the tales that are told,
Here where good fellowship reigns supreme,
    And a fellow just never grows old.
Let us backtrack along life's highways,
    As we relive those pleasures and joys,
Found there along yesterday's byways,
    When as carefree as freckle-faced boys.

With sagas of brookie and rainbow,
    In those beautiful settings we love,
And those big browns feeding at sundown,
    With a caddis hatch swarming above.
Adventures with ringneck and partridge,
    And of hounds as they crisscross the swale,
Or the drone of bullet and cartridge,
    Being fired on the deer's snowy trail.

Yes, here in the glow of the campfire,
    We'll hear stories on many a theme,
For the scent of those pine logs burning,
    Will revive many a cherished dream.
So let's find a seat by the campfire,
    As the stories and tales are told,
Here where good fellowship reigns supreme,
    And a fellow just never grows old.

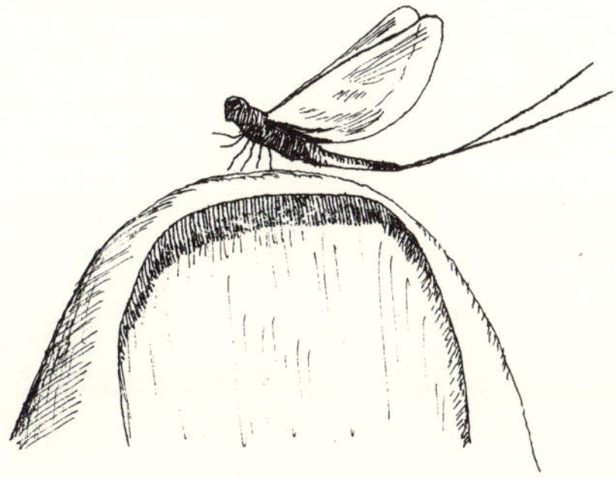

mayfly

Sittin' by the Campfire

Here is a poem which I feel needs little introduction, for the subject is poetry itself: poetry far beyond the scope of a poet's pen to capture; far beyond the realm of mortals, such as I, to portray. It is a setting so beautiful that it leaves one grasping for words to explain its elegance.

Of my many experiences in the outdoors, there is little that equals the radiant beauty of the glowing embers of a campfire in a wooded glen, overlooking a mirrored lake in the wilderness, where a million stars appear to be dancing gracefully o'er the tiny waves, in an unending parade to the sandy beach below.

Perhaps the settings are a little different, but every bit as beautiful: a spot where those pine knots blaze up and spark on the bank of a meandering stream, and the same myriad of stars in the heavens seems so close that one might reach up and grasp them. There is the tranquil murmur of an evening breeze whispering through the pines. Their lofty branches swaying gracefully 'neath the baton of some unseen maestro. Listen to the unending melody of the stream, interrupted occasionally by the splashing of a trout darting to the surface to retrieve some errant moth or fly which had carelessly approached its lair. Hear the song of the catbird and a distant whippoorwill calling to their mates.

Wherever that campfire is located, one will always find a circle of smiling faces caught in its reflection. A place where good fellowship reigns supreme, and life's sorrows and hatreds are a forgotten thing. Man, whether he be prince or pauper, under the spell of the wilderness campfire, will be ushered into that friendly aura of comradeship.

Yes, I believe everything in the world of the great outdoors spells poetry in its greatest form, for in no other environment can one find such splendor created by the greatest artist of them all.

Down through the years I have stored away a multitude of memories gathered from experiences in this beautiful world of nature. Among the finest are those sessions of sittin' by the campfire with that never-ending circle of friends.

So here is my version of "Sittin' by the Campfire." If by chance it creates some heartwarming thought for you, while there by the fireside on a cold winter's evening, I shall feel amply repaid.

Sittin' by the Campfire

When there's rainbow in the skillet,
All cookin' nice and brown,
And there's beauty in the heavens,
Where the sun has just gone down.
There's a session in the offing,
The most peaceful that I know,
Just sittin' by the campfire,
With its warm and friendly glow.

When those mystic evenin' shadows,
Enshroud the camp once more,
An' the boys have finished countin',
"Fifteen-two and fifteen-four."
With those pine logs piled there waitin',
To put on their evenin' show,
When they'll blaze up and sparkle,
With that warm and friendly glow.

What a world for reminiscing,
To relive some cherished dreams,
The happenings of yesteryear,
On those many lakes and streams.
An atmosphere more peaceful,
I am sure I'll never know,
Than sittin' by the campfire,
With its warm and friendly glow.

You seldom hear an unkind word,
They seem so out of place,
And such a thing as unkind thoughts,
Good fellowship will erase.
Where those tiny seeds of friendship,
Seem to blossom forth and grow,
Just sittin' by the campfire,
With its warm and friendly glow.

Hear your buddy there describin',
His one greatest thrill of all,
How that lunker struck a Coachman,
Just below the waterfall.
Say, you sorta get the feelin',
That you're fightin' that big bow,
Just sittin' by the campfire,
With its warm and friendly glow.

In a world so close to heaven,
Just to sit around and plan,
And you seem a whole lot closer,
Toward your fellow man.
Some folks may call it primitive,
But their comforts I'd forego,
To be sittin' by the campfire,
With its warm and friendly glow.

Angler's Lament

Here's a little fishing story,
One perhaps I should not write,
Of the day I went a-fishing,
When the rainbows wouldn't strike.
I have not told my colleagues,
In our great fly-casters' club,
For they would surely brand me,
As a "dunker" or a "dub."

I had started out one evening,
And the weather was just right,
Wind in the best direction,
And the heavens not too bright.
Yes, everything was perfect,
And my spirits light and gay,
As I visualized a limit catch,
When I returned that day.

The spot that I had chosen,
Not very far away,
Was where the river gently turned,
And formed a little bay.
The best hole on the river,
Was many anglers' claim,
And many stories I had heard,
Of its flashing, fighting game.

I approached it very carefully,
As gently there I trod,
Taking every care and caution,
As I set my line and rod.
Then, studying the waters,
A great sight met my eyes,
For the splashes and the ripples,
Said the trout were taking flies.

In tense anticipation,
I chose a caddis fly,
It had proved the most successful,
On my fishing days gone by.
Then casting very carefully,
Out where the trout were feeding,
My lure never fazed them,
They just went on unheeding.

I tried a Royal Coachman,
In all its colors gay,
But those rainbows just ignored it,
And continued at their play.
I tried a White Mosquito,
I tried a Squirrel Tail,
Becoming more and more dejected,
As I saw these lures fail.

I tried out several streamers,
And a dozen other flies,
Retrieving very carefully,
But failed to get a rise.
I was feeling quite despondent,
You know how anglers feel,
When they've done a lot of fishing,
And have an empty creel.

For in those twilight hours,
I really gave my best,
My patience nigh exhausted,
I vowed I'd quit the test.
I detested going back to camp,
And tell the boys I'd flunked,
And hear a lot of kidding,
About the boy that had been skunked.

So I continued fishing,
For several minutes more,
When I spied a can of crawlers,
Abandoned near the shore.
I had never been a dunker,
And fought the urge to try it,
But could those lowly earthworms,
Be on the rainbows' diet?

Fighting with my conscience,
I strung one on my hook,
Being strictly a fly fisherman,
I felt almost like a crook.
I studied there a moment,
As a dunker I'd be classed,
Then summoning my courage,
Half-heartedly I cast.

The bait barely hit the water,
When a streak of red – a flash –
A fighting two-pound rainbow,
Had struck it with a crash!
Tense moments of excitement,
The kind I'll not forget,
Before I brought this beauty,
Into the waiting net.

One thing I discovered,
With my fly rod bent in half,
As out toward the riffles,
My line was streaking fast.
Fish leaping from the water,
A real soul-stirring sight,
Regardless of the bait employed,
You get the same old fight.

And so for thirty minutes,
Those rainbows quickly struck,
The one bait I had so despised,
Had really changed my luck.
None less than thirteen inches,
And each one full of fight,
The limit catch I'd dreamed of,
Filled my soul with great delight.

Please don't class me as a dunker,
But try to understand,
I worship you fly fishermen,
As something fine and grand.
So I'll continue casting flies,
But since that day I've felt,
That it's silly to go fishing,
Without a bait box on my belt.

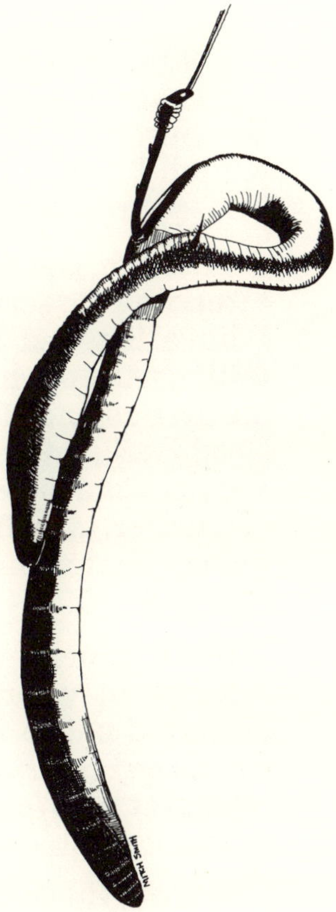

Only He

I have often wondered just what kind of a Christian I really am. I have never aligned myself with any particular church. At times I feel rather silly when asked which church I belong to. Usually my reply is, "All of them." Those three words sum up my Christian beliefs.

Through the years I have enjoyed the pleasure of attending the services of many different denominations. I have listened to the preachings of many different faiths. Although they were varied, the procedure was much the same. The speaker selected a passage from the Good Book, and went on to interpret it in his own way. Very seldom did one's interpretation coincide with that of another, although the vast majority seemed to convey much worthwhile knowledge of Christianity to their followers.

Many times I have sat and listened with profound interest to wonderful sermons by learned men. It mattered not to me which pulpit they were preaching from, the important thing was that they were trying to interpret the Word of God and lead their followers in the paths of righteousness. Who could do more?

Some of these sermons were of the fire and brimstone variety, as the speakers endeavored to frighten their followers into the Christian way of life. While reminiscing over some of these it brings to mind the opening stanza of a fine poem by that world-renowned poet, Robert Service, which follows:

> When the long, long day is over, and the big
> boss gives me my pay,
> I hope it won't be in hell-fire, as some of the
> parsons say,
> And I hope it won't be in heaven, with some
> of the parsons I've met,
> All I want is just quiet, just to rest and
> forget.

I've read this poem many times and always find it rather intriguing. At least it provides plenty of food for meditation.

As far back as I can remember, I've always held an unwavering faith in God. Though I have listened to many sermons expounding His work and sacrifice for us, I am convinced that my great faith in Him stems from the fact that I see Him constantly and feel His presence all about me in His miraculous creations and actions. I find this even more so when I visit that wonderful world of nature.

There in the wilderness, far off the beaten track, I see those towering pines, clusters of shimmering birches, mighty oaks, ferns, flowers, placid lakes, and meandering streams. I could go on and on endeavoring to depict this endless sea of wondrous, natural beauty, but that would be a task far beyond the scope of mortals such as I. All this did not just happen. It is part and parcel of His wonderful plan, and therein lies my unwavering faith.

I recall a discussion we had one night while sitting around the campfire. On this particular occasion there were five in our party. We were encamped on the Manistee River, a short distance below the Cameron Road Bridge. This was a beautiful spot. The fishing from the bridge down to the flats had been very good. The weather, too, had been well nigh perfect. All in all it had been an ideal week.

We had partaken of a fine dinner of rainbow trout that evening. With the dishes cleaned up and the cribbage session over with, we once again congregated around the campfire for our usual discussions on the happenings of the day, comparisons of flies and streams we had fished, and a host of other subjects. The glowing embers of a campfire, on a night such as this, seem to revive cherished memories.

There are two subjects I always try to avoid at a time like this, religion and politics. Either one could develop into some rather heated discussions, especially among men of different faiths and ideals. But on this beautiful night, quite unknowingly, the subject drifted into religious channels, as one of the boys began extolling the greatness of God. After a short discussion on the subject, another asked, "How can we be sure there is a God? After all, nobody has ever seen Him."

I was more than a little dumbfounded at my friend's doubt, especially in this beautiful setting. Following a moment of contemplation, I looked over at him and said, "Bob, just look around you at all His great creations and let your eyes supply the answer. Surely this splendor all about us will erase any doubt from your mind. I recall a short stanza from the Good Book – I believe it is in Psalms – which states, 'The heavens declare the glory of God; and the firmament showeth his handiwork.' And I imagine that it is work such as this that those lines refer to. How anyone could doubt such a thing is beyond me."

For the moment I thought I had convinced him, but such was not the case. He continued, "I agree, all this is very interesting, but I'm sure you'll agree that man, too, deserves a great deal of credit. Take into consideration all the marvelous creations that men have come up with to ease the burdens of life; material things which make everything so much better for us all."

At the moment this statement seemed to be a rather persuasive argument, as I sat there and pondered over the amazing progress we had witnessed over the past fifty years. Almost immediately this argument became overshadowed as a new line of reasoning came to me. I replied, "Bob, about the only things that our fellowmen have given us are those that the good Lord has allowed them to in order to ease our path. Can't you see He merely uses the brain of man as a transfer point and implants in man's mind the formulas for these wonderful creations? After all, God created man in the beginning and, such being the case, I'm sure you will agree that He has the power to control our destiny. Certainly God gives man the power and the ability to pass on to us many wonderful creations, but He also retains the greatest formulas of all in order to prove to us just how helpless we are without Him.

"Let me illustrate my point. For argument's sake, let us call upon the greatest scientists in all the world and supply them with the finest laboratories with every chemical and ingredient known to mankind. Even go beyond that and give them the seeds for their analysis of the product, and tell them to produce a seed which will grow a stalk of grain, or a flower, or perhaps a tree. You will find that without the actual seed given to us by our good Lord, they will be completely helpless. This is but one example of our helplessness without Him. I could go on and mention others, but I'm sure this one example will erase any doubt regarding His great powers."

This ended our rather interesting discussion on the subject, as Bob conceded that I had convinced him of the powers of a glorious God. With that, this very intriguing conversation ended. The subject once more returned to plans for the morrow, the best flies to use, the weather, and other subjects more conducive to the glow of a wilderness campfire.

The hour was nearing midnight when I finally crawled into my sleeping bag, and long after the boys had gone to sleep, I lay there pondering over that interesting session by the fire. It had provided me with plenty of food for thought, and also the idea for the following poem, which I have titled, "Only He."

Only He

I peered into the heart of a rose,
  And I saw God resting there,
As part of those beautiful petals,
  With fragrance beyond compare.
Who could create such a splendid thing?
  The thought then occurred to me,
And I heard a voice close to my heart,
  As it whispered, "Only He."

I gazed one day at the might of an oak,
  As it seemed to brush the sky,
And pausing in awesome wonder there,
  I could see God standing by.
And a surge of warmth engulfed my heart,
  As my soul felt clean and free,
Who could create such strength and beauty?
  Said the same voice, "Only He."

I paused one day by a rustic bridge,
  Far off in a wooded glen,
And reflecting in those waters there,
  I could see God once again.
From whence came this Eden-like beauty,
  As far as the eye could see?
Those rippling waters there below,
  Seemed to whisper, "Only He."

As I looked across a field of grain,
  Swaying gently in the air,
And pausing, spellbound by its beauty,
  I could see God standing there.
Though man had planted those tiny seeds,
  Who had wrought this golden sea?
That beautiful voice deep in my heart,
  Seemed to whisper, "Only He."

Rainbow Bill's Lament

The majority of poems in this book were inspired by personal experiences, campfire reminiscences, or perhaps a beautiful locale, but in the following poem, "Rainbow Bill's Lament," I have endeavored to create a situation by using a little of each.

The characters are all real people, either fellows I have had the pleasure of meeting, or others I have heard about during a session by the campfire. Naturally, in a poem of this type, I have refrained from naming the towns in which they reside, or the rivers and streams where they usually stalk their game. Obviously, I have no desire to incur their displeasure by bringing them together in a plot of this nature.

But let me repeat, the characters are all genuine. "Rainbow" Bill lived in a cabin on one of Michigan's famous trout streams and was noted for his ability as a trout fisherman. Many times I have heard the remark, "If 'Rainbow' Bill can't get 'em, then what chance have we got?" Thus, I gathered from the many stories I heard commending his angling knowledge that he must have been in a class by himself as far as trout fishing was concerned.

The "Fishing Parson" would spend as much of his time as possible along the trout streams in and around his parish. I heard about the "Fishing Parson" through an old-time friend of mine, whom I will refer to as Joe.

Joe was a native of a small town in northern Michigan, and sad to say, he was about the greatest violator in town when it came to fishing, strictly a meat fisherman. Joe at times would confide to me, "You know, I never carry more than a limit of trout in my creel, but that's not saying how many I actually take home." He seemed to be quite proud of his ability to violate the game laws, truly a braggart type with little or no fear of the game wardens.

The following conversation, which I overheard one day between Joe and the chief game warden of the district, may serve to illustrate my point. This had taken place one day at a gas station where Joe worked part-time. The warden had pulled up to one of the pumps and Joe came out of the station to serve him. The conversation went something like this:

"Hi, Warden, how's business?"

"About the same as always, Joe. How's things going with you?"

"Tolerable, tolerable," Joe replied. "How many?" inquired Joe, removing the hose from the pump.

"Fill her up, Joe. Got quite a lot of traveling to do."

"Been catchin' any violators lately, warden?"

"No," replied the warden, "guess you're about the only one that's still in business. By the way, have you been doing any fishing lately?"

"Whenever I get a chance, warden. Was over to the creek yesterday for awhile. Got about twenty-two altogether. Some may have been a little undersize, but you know me, warden, I never throw any back. Those small ones taste just as good as the big ones. No siree, I never throw any back."

"You may be kiddin', Joe, but knowing you as well as I do, you could be right. Probably you think you're pretty damn smart, but I'll get you with the goods one of these days, and I'll guarantee they'll throw the book at you when that happens, mark my words."

"Well, warden, you been tryin' for the last twenty years an' you haven't caught me yet, so I ain't gonna worry too much."

Thus ended a conversation which had begun affably and wound up on rather a terse note. Joe appeared to derive a great deal of pleasure out of his contempt for the game laws, and more so for those fellows whose job it was to enforce them.

Several times I had tried to point out to Joe the error of his ways. I stressed the fact that by taking those small trout he was only spoiling fishing for the future by not allowing them to mature into legal-sized fish. I also pointed out the tremendous cost involved in raising trout and stocking the streams, but all to no avail. He was so set in his ways that no amount of preaching on my part was going to change him. About the only way I managed to keep him a little bit in line was by insisting on quitting when I realized he was nearing his limit on days when fishing was productive.

But to get back to the Fishing Parson. He, too, was a friend of Joe's and Joe appeared to be a little jealous of the parson's ability to take trout. Whenever he mentioned the parson to me, I seemed to detect a note of admiration in his voice.

The Fishing Parson's home was just north of town not far from the conservation dam. This was an artificial dam constructed by the conservation department and stocked with legal-sized trout. At that time, legal trout had to be seven inches in length, with a limit of ten fish for one day's catch; whereas the rules governing the dam was a minimum length of ten inches, five trout per day on flies only.

Joe and I had visited this dam on several occasions without success. I think we had tried about every size and pattern of fly in the book, but could not seem to raise a trout. Joe claimed there were no trout in the dam, deciding that the trout were either going back upstream or escaping through the dam and heading downstream. Personally, I lost interest in the place and concentrated my efforts on more productive spots.

About one year later, when I stopped in town to eat, I met Joe in the restaurant. After rehashing old times he confided to me that he finally had found the secret of taking trout at the conservation dam. Taking his fly box from his pocket, he selected a fly and handed it to me. "That's the baby right there. Hell, I must have taken twenty or thirty trout on that one alone." I examined the fly, endeavoring to recognize it, but it was different from any that I had seen. But then there were probably hundreds of those. "What's it called?" I asked.

"Hell, you can't buy them," Joe answered, "I got that one from the Fishing Parson. Gettin' kind of chewed up. I've tried around town to have it copied, but they don't seem to have the right materials for tyin' them. I'll try and get a couple more from the parson."

"How did you manage to get this one?" I asked.

"Well, it was kind of funny," Joe replied. "I had spent a couple of hours one morning down at the dam, but it was the same old story. Not a rise. So I packed up and headed for home. Well, while driving past the parson's place I noticed him outside cleaning some fish. They looked like pretty good ones to me, so I pulled into his driveway to get a closer look. Boy, he had five real nice ones, all around eleven or twelve inches. After the customary small talk I complimented him on his fine catch and asked him where he got them. I was really dumbfounded when he informed me that he had taken them at the conservation dam. It was pretty hard for me to swallow, but him bein' a parson I figgered he wouldn't lie about them, but I was still kinda doubtful. I told him I was just on my way home, and had spent a couple of hours down at the dam without a rise, plus all the other times I had visited the dam without success."

"That's funny," he replied, "I usually do rather well down there."

"Becoming more skeptical by the minute, I asked him whether I might accompany him on his next trip and much to my surprise he replied, 'Well, I'm having company over tonight for a fish fry, and I could use a few more trout. I actually caught these last evening, so I suppose I could take a few more today without breaking any laws. If you care to we could go back down there now.' I really jumped at the opportunity, and in a short time we were at the dam assembling our gear. I asked the parson which part of the dam he preferred to fish. He replied, 'One spot is just about as good as another, so you go ahead and fish where the water is a little deeper.' The parson commenced casting about fifty feet below. I checked my fly box, tryin' to figure which one to use and finally decided on a Coachman. Hell, I had used every thing before, an' they all appeared to be about the same.

"I probably had made about five or six casts when I happened to glance around at the parson and, lo and behold, he was reelin' in a trout. It looked like a pretty nice one too. That made me feel pretty good, as I figgered they'd finally begun to rise. I made a few more casts with the Coachman, then switched to an Adams. I had made several casts with this when, believe it or not, I noticed the parson reelin' in another trout. That was two in about ten minutes. I was really putting everything I had into it now, as I contemplated getting a rise any minute. This went on for several minutes when I glanced around at the parson again. Yes, you guessed it. He was in the act of nettin' another fish. Boy, that was really frustratin'. He was makin' me look bad. I tried several more patterns and sizes but still nary a rise, and it seemed every time I looked at the parson he was reeling in a trout. Finally I noticed him taking down his rod and packin' up. I figgered he was ready to go, so I reeled in too and walked over to where be was waitin'.

"'Do any good?' he asked. I replied that I had got my usual goose egg.

"'I know you got your limit, Parson,' I said, peering into his creel, 'but tell me just what kind of a fly were you using?'"

"'Why this fly here,' he replied. 'It's a gadget I tie myself, so it's really got no name. Slightly resembles the Coachman. I've found it to be most productive. Here, take this one and try it. We have plenty of time and I don't want you to quit empty handed.'"

"Well, sir, that was the fly right there and it's really a honey. I tied it on and went back to the spot I had just left and on the second cast I got a beautiful strike an' netted a twelve-incher. To make a long story short, within thirty minutes I had taken five dandies. I figgered on continuing fishin' when my luck was runnin' that good, but the parson said, 'Well, that one gives you a limit so we have to quit. You may keep that fly, being as you have done so well with it.' I really hated to quit, but you know how the parson is about keepin' the rules, so we packed up and went home.

"I dropped the parson off and went home and cleaned those fish and put them in the refrigerator. Then I took off for the dam again and inside of an hour I had five more. Then after supper I went back and got seven more. Boy, seventeen trout in one day at a place that I figgered was no good. Well, that's the secret of takin' trout at the conservation dam. I am sure I can get some more of those flies from the parson."

That was the story of the Fishing Parson, and bringing these two fine fishermen together in a rather humorous episode was the inspiration created for the poem "Rainbow Bill's Lament."

Rainbow Bill's Lament

"It just about freezes your britches,"
Said Bill as he laid down his pole,
"I've stood in that stream by the hour,
And fished every inch of that hole.
Tried every trick that I know of,
Used every last fly in the kit,
But still it's the same old story,
Just can't get that lunker to hit.

"I saw him again this evenin',
And oh what a beauty is he,
Leapin' clear out of the water,
Less than ten feet in front of me.
Six pounds or better, I'll warrant,
May even go seven or eight,"
Bill swore when his buddy said something,
About using the wrong kind of bait.

"I'll get him, you betcha, I'll get him,
It's going to take patience and skill,
But I promise to land that baby,
Or my name's not Rainbow Bill."
As the campfire embers were dying,
And midnight was fast drawing nigh,
Bill squatted there in the lamplight,
Conjuring a new kind of fly.

Back on the stream before sunup,
Absorbed in his favorite chore,
Casting, retrieving and casting,
With no better luck than before.
Once in a while he'd get rises,
A few trout of measuring size,
Just serving to whet his passion,
In his quest for that special prize.

With Bill it became an obsession,
Smitten hard by lust and desire,
Preparing, working and planning,
In those evenings around the campfire.
Bill planned to have the trout mounted,
Had a spot picked out in his den,
And really blasphemed his buddy,
For using the simple term, "When?"

And so it went throughout the week,
With Bill living there on the stream,
Striving to find that treasured rise,
To crown his one wonderful dream.
It happened on that final day,
We had breakfast and packed our gear,
And just as we'd all expected,
Our friend Bill was nowhere near.

He'd been on the stream since daybreak,
For today it meant do or die,
And as we tarried there waiting,
The Fishin' Parson happened by.
He preached at the church in the valley,
We had met several times before,
And outside of preaching the gospel,
Catching trout was his favorite chore.

He paused to pass the time of day,
As most sportsmen usually do,
Bill told him about that lunker,
And of the ordeal he'd been through.
Describing the many flies and lures,
He had used to promote a hit,
And the parson smiled and nodded,
As though he'd stretched the facts a bit.

Poor Bill bemoaned his failures,
As this humble picture struck,
"Say, while I take a breather, sir,
Just go ahead and try your luck."
The parson stepped into the stream,
Adjusting his fly rod and line,
While Bill was muttering something,
Of it being a waste of time.

"It matters not which fly you use,
I've tried 'em all in every size,
You'll do as well selecting one,
If you merely close your eyes."
"I have but one," the parson said,
"It's a gadget I tie myself,
Slightly resembles the Coachman,
But I've named it the Dancing Elf."

The parson made his opening cast,
About as perfect as could be,
And the way he played that tiny fly,
Was a beautiful sight to see.
Making a very slow retrieve,
His line gracefully twirled once more,
And the fly danced o'er the riffles,
Then slowly arched toward the shore.

It was then that lunker hit it,
Like all Hades had broken loose,
Struck with all the frenzied fury,
That these great fighting fish produce.
It came leaping from the water,
Fighting to throw that tiny fly,
Dived again with a mighty splash,
As those moments went fleeting by.

I quickly glanced around at Bill,
As he stumbled over a rock,
His face wore the gaunt expression,
Of a man who had entered shock.
Back in the stream the fight went on,
As that rainbow writhed and coiled,
The waters of that tranquil pool,
With all that fury, fairly boiled.

Now he's streaking for the rapids,
Then turns and darts toward the shore,
Again leaping from the water,
Fighting to throw that fly once more.
The time seemed like countless ages,
Before the final stage was set,
And I watched the Fishin' Parson,
Finally lead him to his net.

He removed him very gently,
Held him high that we all might see,
Then with an air of nonchalance,
Stooped down and calmly set him free.
Poor Bill was ranting and raving,
As he watched that prize swim away,
With the Parson's explanation,
"I'd caught all I could use today."

This happened many years ago,
But the fellows are talking still,
Of the day the Fishin' Parson,
Broke the heart of Rainbow Bill.

Joe's Error

We sat around the cabin,
As we swapped a tale or two,
Those happenings of yesteryear,
While we quaffed a little brew.
'Twas quite a motley gathering,
With our spirits rather high,
Much like when they are flavored,
With a little Scotch and rye.

Yes, all the boys were happy,
You no doubt guess the reason,
'Twas the eve of an adventure,
Another great deer season.
We heard about the deer cinch,
Quite a unique sort of trap,
Most hunters know about it,
So I'll not go into that.

I said we all were happy,
That is, all excepting one,
Joe sat there in a corner,
And, as usual, looking glum.
Not much at conversation,
A retiring sort of guy,
Very much like a martini,
And I mean one plenty dry.

At last I turned and asked him,
How bird hunting was last fall,
He answered, "How should I know,
With no chance to go at all?"
"Don't you always go with Bill?"
I asked inquisitively,
Joe replied, "I always used to,
But I think he's peeved at me.

"The last time that I went along,
It was just a-breakin' day,
When I spied a big cock pheasant,
From the car along the way.
Though it was violatin',
And I had not done it before,
I let go with both barrels,
But my aim was plenty poor."

"Why should Bill be mad at that?"
Drew this answer from the clown,
"Before I shot, I plumb forgot,
To roll the window down."

No Fishing

I one time was invited,
By Paul, a friend of mine,
To join him on a fishing trip,
To play the hook and line.
It didn't take much coaxing,
We soon were on our way,
And like fellows going fishing,
Our hearts were light and gay.

Up to the northern regions,
Land of lakes and streams,
Truly a sportsman's paradise,
A background for his dreams.
It was here that I met Shorty,
Whom Paul introduced with pride,
And claimed that our friend Shorty,
Was as good as any guide.

Well, we didn't do much waiting,
And were on our way once more,
To a spot Shorty had selected,
As a likely place to score.
We trolled the deepest waters,
For muskellunge and pike,
We trolled the so-called good spots,
But didn't get a strike.

We still fished by the hour,
Live minnows were our bait,
Paul complained to Shorty,
"There are no fish in the lake."
We tried our luck at casting,
As the sun began to set,
But our score remained at zero,
For nothing did we get.

"It's mighty strange," said Shorty,
As we headed home that night,
"To fish a lake so full of fish,
And never get a bite.
But tomorrow is another day,
There's another spot I know,
Where I always get some dandies,
Every time I go."

And so for several days we fished,
With Shorty as our guide,
The fact that we had caught no fish,
Had kind of hurt his pride.
I heard him say to Paul one night,
In a kidding sort of way,
"That Jonesie here must be a jinx,
For the fish to act this way."

I conceded that he must be right,
But then I pointed out,
I was never a lake fisherman,
My specialty was trout.
"That settles it," said Shorty,
"I gather what you mean,
Tomorrow bright and early,
We'll head out for a stream."

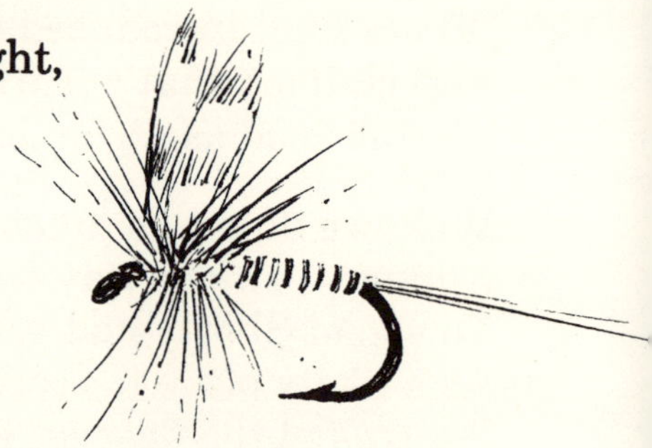
mosquito

As we parked our car at daybreak,
We knew the stream was near,
For as we set our rods and reels,
Its waters we could hear.
"Now here's the plan," said Shorty,
"It's the best way I have found,
Jonesie here, fish upstream,
Paul and I, fish down."

"Go upstream half a mile,
Before you turn about,
You'll surely have your limit,
By then I have no doubt."
Instead of starting at the bridge,
As many would have done,
I took a trail down through the brush,
Almost on the run.

I made a strike on my first cast,
And hooked one measuring size,
I creeled that seven incher,
Quite happy with my prize.
Another cast, another strike,
This one measured nine,
After days of getting none at all,
I considered this was fine.

Two hours of glorious fishing,
A limit in the creel,
From seven to eighteen inches,
Had made the day ideal.
I cleaned the fish and started back,
There was nothing more to do,
I decided Paul and Shorty,
Must have their limits too.

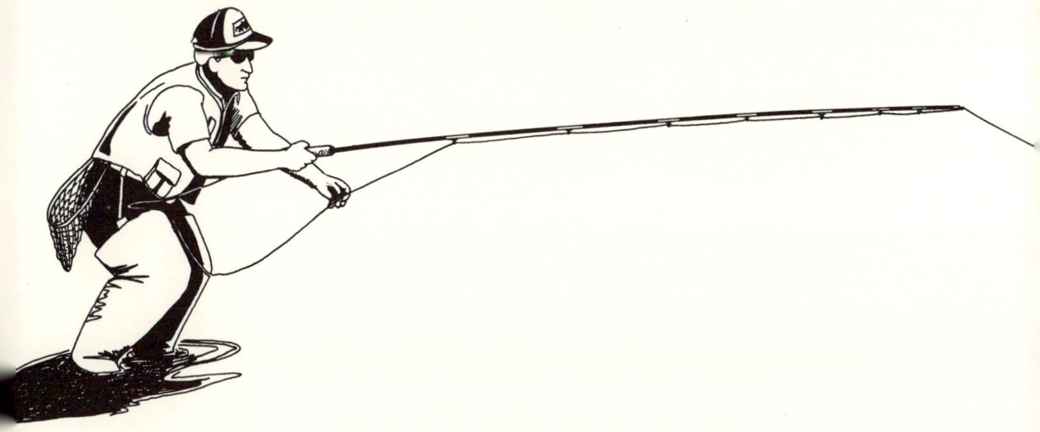

They were waiting at the car,
That day as I arrived,
They surely caught their limit,
In good time, I surmised.
"Any luck?" asked Shorty,
I mentioned it was fine,
Shorty winked at Paul and said,
"Now don't hand us that line."

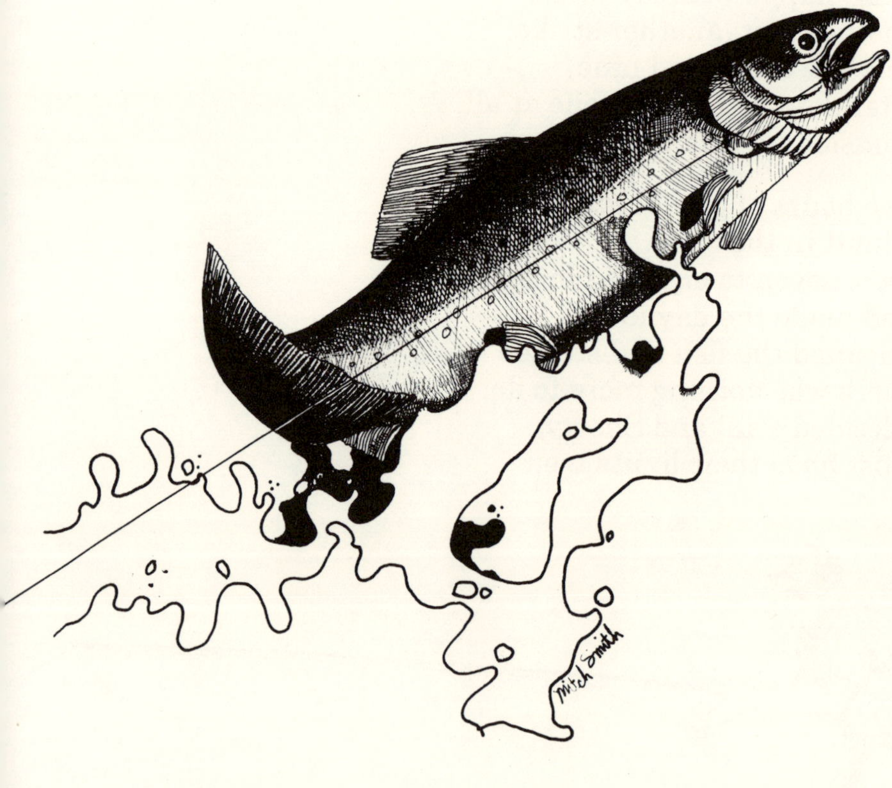

Camp Cook

Here's a little poem dedicated to that congenial chap who, by choice or nomination, elects to practice his culinary arts on the boys in camp. Whether the food served is good or otherwise, he is usually the recipient of many good-natured compliments for his efforts. In the world of the great outdoors a fellow usually has the appetite of a barefoot boy, and regardless of the cooking, almost everything tastes much like a blue plate special.

As far back as I can remember, it seems the task of preparing the meals in camp has ever been my lot. In those early days, with my young sons along, I had no choice. But somehow with the passing years, probably through experience acquired in this field, the nomination of chef seems to remain with me.

No doubt some fellows will consider this a rather menial task on a fishing or hunting trip. It isn't really when taking into consideration that you seldom have to wash any dishes or pots and pans. You will always find some other brave individual who will volunteer for that chore. Personally, I'd rather cook than clean up after the meal is completed.

Then again, when a fellow elects to do the cooking, he usually takes great pride in his efforts and endeavors, certain that those trout are cooked to a turn, along with all the trimmings. He is well rewarded with compliments and smiles of appreciation as the platters are cleaned.

Then comes another rewarding moment in the life of a camp cook. I refer to that beautiful hour at dawn. Usually I make a practice of rising a little earlier than the boys in order to have breakfast started before they crawl out of their sleeping bags. That way they may get a good, early start in their quest for those wily trout. What better way to begin the day than a piping hot breakfast. The aroma of perking coffee permeates the air, in a setting that can do it the justice it deserves.

I think that every moment spent camped on a good trout stream is heaven itself. But were I asked to name the most peaceful moment of them all, I believe I should name that hour just before dawn. A time when the old sun is still struggling to crest those distant pines.

I probably could name more thrilling hours, such as the time when you're wading the waters of the stream around sundown, with a caddis hatch swarming above and trout breaking the surface all about you. Or perhaps the time when that fine brookie laying there 'neath a submerged log happens to spot your fly drifting lazily along the surface and comes darting up to retrieve it, and those never-to-be-forgotten moments which follow as it leaps again and again from the waters in order to throw the pesky thing. Yes, it's times such as these that give the trout fisherman that little something extra in life.

With all this, I'll still name that hour before dawn as the best: a time when the world about you begins to awaken, with those final plaintive calls of the whippoor-will, the sharp tattooing of a woodpecker somewhere across the stream as he, too, is busy seeking breakfast at the beginning of this brand-new day. The early rays of the sun filter through the trees bathing the splendor all about you with alternating casts of silver and gold as it gathers in the glistening dew.

Just about this time, the parade of the birds begins. They truly are a curious lot, flying singly or in pairs, flitting around in the branches above, cocking their heads from side to side, endeavoring to decipher just what kind of monsters are these things called men and what right have they to invade our fair domain? Usually, after satisfying their curiosity, they will oblige with an early morning serenade which conveys the message that all is well. There are times when those beautiful notes are taken up by hosts of others, blending their voices in their own inimitable way, giving a fellow that warm feeling of being accepted.

Yes, the peacefulness of dawn in the woods is something indescribable, with that unspoiled splendor all about you. The tantalizing scent of the evergreens permeates the air, when those beautiful trees have donned their finest gowns and their branches are tipped with a lighter shade of green, giving them the appearance of a multitude of Christmas candles and adding so much to their natural grandeur. There below, stretched across the forest floor, as far as the eye can see, is a beautiful carpet of ferns, wild flowers, vines and patches of wild cherry blossoms. A gracious God is truly a wonderful decorator. Man's efforts, in comparison, are mediocre.

With all this in mind, is it any wonder why I so enjoy these peaceful hours preceding dawn? It was in this beautiful setting that I endeavored to record my impressions in words with the poem titled, "Camp Cook."

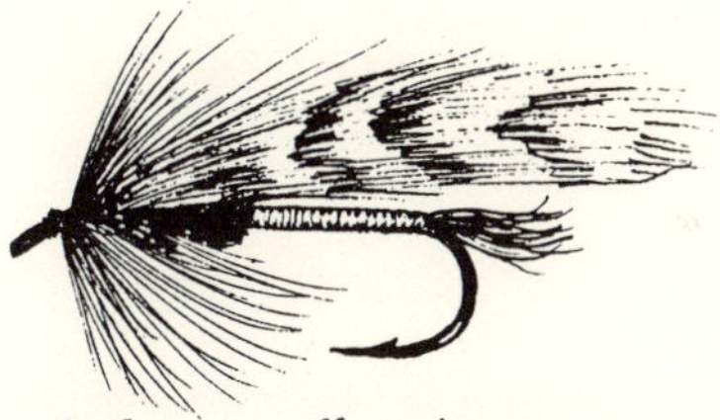

dark spruce fly . streamer

Camp Cook

It's great to sip your coffee
In the shadow of the pines,
When the dew is still a-glistenin'
On the birches and the vines;
With your buddies still a-sleepin'
Waitin' for the break o' day,
Probably dreamin' of the pleasure
Which was found there yesterday.

It's great to sip your coffee
While you're sortin' out those flies,
Tryin' to separate the best ones
From among the wets an' dries;
With the chirpin' of a cricket
Who's impatient with delay,
An' callin' on the Lord above
To bring on another day.

It's great to sip your coffee
Where a stream goes flowin' by,
And you kind-a hear a splashin'
As a rainbow takes a fly;
There's a joy beyond description
Which engulfs the soul within,
And you find yourself a-prayin'
Some new glories to begin.

It's great to sip your coffee
As the sunrise filters through,
An' seems to say, "Good morning"
While it gathers in the dew;
It's time to heat the griddle
For the flapjacks an' the ham,
Yep, it's time to call your buddies
An' this brand new day to plan.

Paradise

Paradise

I suppose almost everyone has his own idea of paradise and has a pretty fair conception of what it is like. But being a trout fisherman, I have endeavored to explain in the following poem my idea of a spot that comes mighty close to being paradise.

So picture with me a weather-beaten cabin by the side of a winding road, nothing much to look at. As you arrive there in the spring, the windows are all boarded up in order to withstand the rigors of winter, the same way you reluctantly left them on that final visit the previous season. No, it's nothing much to look at, but oh the wonderful memories it revives of fine trout taken in that early morning session a short distance from the cabin.

Remember the time you downed that twelve-point buck, not more than half a mile away? That was really something. What a time the boys had that night in the old cabin, as kind of a celebration. Yes, it might look kind of old and tumbledown, but with all those memories locked within, it's paradise to you.

Paradise might be that rustic campsite there near the end of a winding road. You remember that little clearing situated among clusters of birches and pines on a knoll overlooking the stream. What memories it revives. The rising of fine brooks and rainbows at daybreak, at that hour when the old sun is still struggling to crest those tall pines, and the forest about you comes alive with voices of its creatures as they flutter and scurry about on important errands of this brand-new day.

Then comes that beautiful trill of the robin somewhere up there in the branches of that tall birch, notes blending into each other in perfect rhythm. While there in another tree, a short distance away, a brown thrasher flits from one branch to another doing his best to imitate that beautiful melody with a jumble of notes of his own. The robin, cocking his head from one side to the other, patiently listens to the thrasher's version, then flies off in disgust.

Yes, it's truly a wonderful spot to be in to greet the brand-new day. This is my idea of a world which comes very close to being paradise, suffused with an Eden-like beauty, where the noise of the city with all its din and clamor is completely forgotten.

Planning a vacation to such a spot revives so many wonderful memories. It's a great feeling when the time arrives and the car is loaded with your treasured gear. You finally head down the highway, leaving the city far behind. The traffic begins to thin out and business places become farther and farther apart. The electrifying moment arrives when you finally turn onto that winding road along the river, and all those winter dreams seem to burst forth into a wonderful reality. It is this feeling which prompted me to write the poem, "Paradise."

Paradise

Where the noise of the city fades away,
As the road begins to wind,
And those cares and troubles of yesterday,
Are lost on the trail behind.
Where the pine cones carpet the wooded hill,
With the forest folk at play,
And the heart will shed every man-made ill,
With the birth of this carefree day.

Let me pull the shade on the world without,
And turn to that world within,
With its air of peacefulness all about,
And devoid of greed and sin.
Let me breathe once more the nectared air,
Where the pine trees brush the sky,
Where God's handiwork is everywhere,
And His heaven seems nearby.

Where the starlit nights are oh so still,
O'er a world that knows no wrong,
Where the sunrise beckons the songbird's trill,
And the world awakes to song.
Let me ever seek those carefree days,
And the peacefulness I'll find,
Where the noise of the city fades away,
And the road begins to wind.

The Slumbering Stream

A beautiful lady slumbers today,
    Here in this crystallized glen;
Her wonderful voice, but a whisper now,
    Vibrates in my heart again.
No power can quell such a splendid thing,
    And no mute could still your song;
Which has made all men who have paused to hear,
    A happy and carefree throng.

Slumber on, fair goddess of paradise,
    For God has decreed you rest;
Sleep with those beautiful blossoms and leaves,
    And the empty songbird's nest.
Sleep on in your sparkling ermine gown,
    While your home is quiet and still;
'Neath the emerald cloak of those evergreens,
    That watch o'er you from the hill.

'Til the loving hand of a gracious God,
    Will bid you wake once more;
And your voice will blend with songbird's trill,
    More beautiful than before.

Indications

The maples sprout in tender bud,
    The robin's on the wing,
Returning from those warmer climes,
    Sweet melodies to sing.
The groundhog seeks his shadow,
    The brown bear takes a stroll,
Tender blossoms raise their head,
    Beside a streamside knoll.

The squirrel, fox and chipmunk,
    Dart in springtime ecstasy,
As the forest is awakened,
    To the songbird's symphony.
Sweet arbutus and sweet fern,
    The awakened columbine,
Forget-me-nots and marigold,
    The perfume of the pine.

All herald the approach of spring,
    While blossoms by the score,
Appear like many throw rugs,
    All across the forest floor.
Speckled trout in a crystal pool,
    The sharptail's mating call,
But grandpa patching his fishing boots,
    Is the greatest sign of all.

Little Eden

There's a spot there in the woodlands,
    Just a tiny sheltered glen,
So Eden-like and peaceful,
    Unspoiled by hands of men.
With clouds in fleecy echelons,
    Drifting lazily above,
O'er a world that spells contentment,
    In an atmosphere of love.

Where tall and whispering pine trees,
    Stretch their arms toward the sky,
And a tiny brook goes singing,
    An unending lullaby.
To lay upon its shady banks,
    To close my eyes and dream,
In a world so close to heaven,
    Ever peaceful and serene.

To dream of those things I'm proud of,
    Banish the ones to regret,
Divorced from my worldly labors,
    To rest, dear Lord, and forget.

trillium

The Forest

June, and the forest is newly gowned,
With beautiful landscapes all around.
Quaint settings which God alone prescribes,
Far beyond man's power to describe.
Beyond the artist's skill to capture,
Breathtaking grandeur to enrapture.

So staunch and sturdy, the mighty oak,
Nestling there in its leafy cloak.
Could the maples and those lofty pine,
Be jealous of splendor such as thine?
Resplendent in beauty of their own,
Adding so much to their forest home.

Each flower and vine, and all else that grows,
At God's command don their finest clothes.
Just to tarry in admiration there,
A world of enchantment everywhere.
In reverence I ask the reason why,
Through winter months must this fade and die?

Comes an answering voice which seems to say,
"I've the power to give and take away."
There's some who scoff and claim for reason,
All plant life dies in winter's season.
With the forest barren, bleak and bare,
As a soul burdened with great despair.

To be sere and slumber until spring,
When with warmer nights those buds will bring.
"'Twas thus," they'll say since the world began,
A fact which is known to every man.
But on the bleakest of winter days,
They'll emerge in glory to amaze.

Just pause there after a winter's rain,
In dazzling splendor the forest flames.
The goddess of beauty nestled there,
In a maze of crystal everywhere.
When the trees stand forth in great array,
As diamond plumes in grand display.

From mighty giants, to the humble stems,
In shimmering garb of glittering gems.
And where'er you look the scene unfurls,
Like emeralds, rhinestones, priceless pearls.
With settings to thwart the hand of man,
While dwarfing his effort and his plan.

His greatest pageants, his finest art,
But nothing like this can he impart.
Rare grandeur to alter hate to love,
By the master painter there above.
Like a memo from the Great Creator –
Have faith in Me, there is none greater.

Thrills of Life

Just as I thrill to a rising trout,
    When a caddis hatch is swarming,
I also thrill to a fragrant rose,
    With a beautiful June day dawning.
To the tangy scent of a stalwart pine,
    In the wake of a summer shower,
To those placid lakes and winding streams,
    And each delicate woodland flower.

I also thrill to the songbird's trill,
    As it floats from the forest glen,
To the marigolds and daffodils,
    Finely etched by the Master's pen.
Let me tread that path far from life's wrath,
    With it's hatred and cares and strife,
To the peace I'll find in a world entwined,
    In those wonderful things of life.

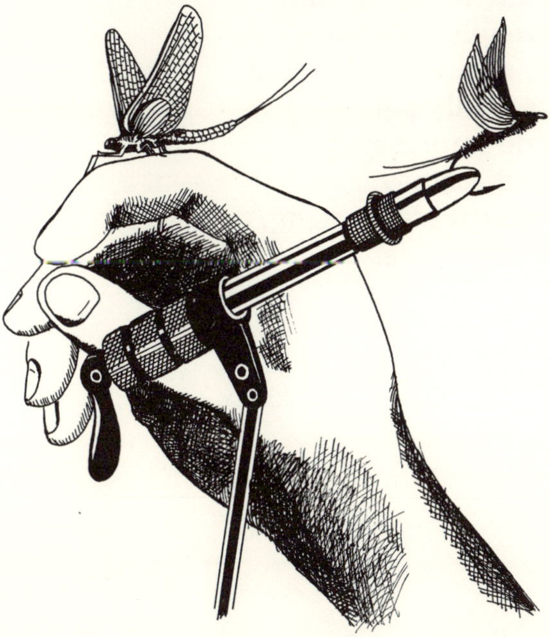

The Making of a Tree

The idea from the songbird's call,
    The fragrance from a flower,
The staunchness from a mountain tall,
    And shade from the vesper hour.
Gay colors from a twilight sky,
    To provide the autumn hue,
Rustic glow from the moon on high,
    And the freshness from the dew.

The stillness from a starlit night,
    The stem from a tulip tall,
Height was gauged to the songbird's flight,
    The leaf from an ivied wall.
The swirling art from a lacy scroll,
    To be etched against the sky,
The contours from a grassy knoll,
    Where a brook flows slowly by.

The whisper from a winding stream,
    Meandering through the glen,
The blueprint from a cherished dream,
    And etched by a Godly pen.
Standing stately and impressing,
    For man's joy and ecstasy,
He then crowned it with his blessing,
    And God had made a tree.

That's Livin'.

When you drive down that loggin' road once more,
That's Livin'.
You're nearin' the spot where you camped before,
That's Livin'.
On a stream which is noted for its trout,
Just the gamest of fish, beyond a doubt,
With an air of enchantment all about,
That's Livin'.

And when you all pitch in to set up camp,
That's Livin'.
When you erect the tent, and fuel the lamp,
That's Livin'.
Where a beautiful stream goes flowing by,
Giving solace to both the heart and eye,
With your hand just itchin' to cast a fly,
That's Livin'.

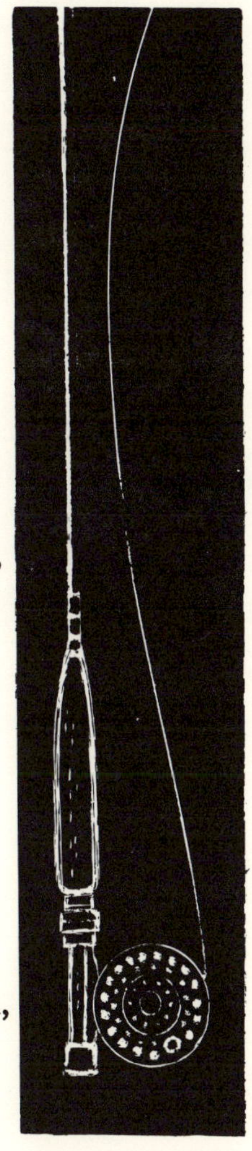

As the shadows of evenin' begin to fall,
That's Livin'.
When you hear the whippoorwill's mating call,
That's Livin'.
When you gather 'round the fire at night,
'Neath a million stars all shinin' bright,
And you reminisce, an' you puff your pipe,
That's Livin'.

There on your cot with the canvas above,
That's Livin'.
Givin' thanks to God for these things you love,
That's Livin'.
Cloaked 'neath those whispering pines so high,
Watch the campfire embers just fade and die,
As the stream below goes bubblin' by,
That's Livin'.

To awake when the sun begins to rise,
That's Livin'.
Those cheerful greetings from regular guys,
That's Livin'.
You see the best in your fellow man,
As you laugh, an' jest, an' talk an' plan,
While the bacon's sizzlin' in the pan,
That's Livin'.

When you pick your favorite rod and reel,
That's Livin'.
When you don your boots and hook your creel,
That's Livin'.
When you pause to check that box of flies,
And ponder the question "Wets or Dries?"
Then you're off in quest of that treasured rise,
That's Livin'.

With your heart and soul brimful of joy,
That's Livin'.
An' you're carefree as a barefoot boy,
That's Livin'.
What matter if fishin' is good or bad,
Your step is light, and your heart is glad,
When you thank God for the fun you've had,
That's Livin'.

Boyhood

Boyhood Dreams

When I was a little lad,
    A-fishing off the quay,
I yearned to see romantic spots,
    So very far away.
But now I've grown to manhood,
    And can sate my urge to roam,
I find my heart is sated,
    By a place called Home Sweet Home.

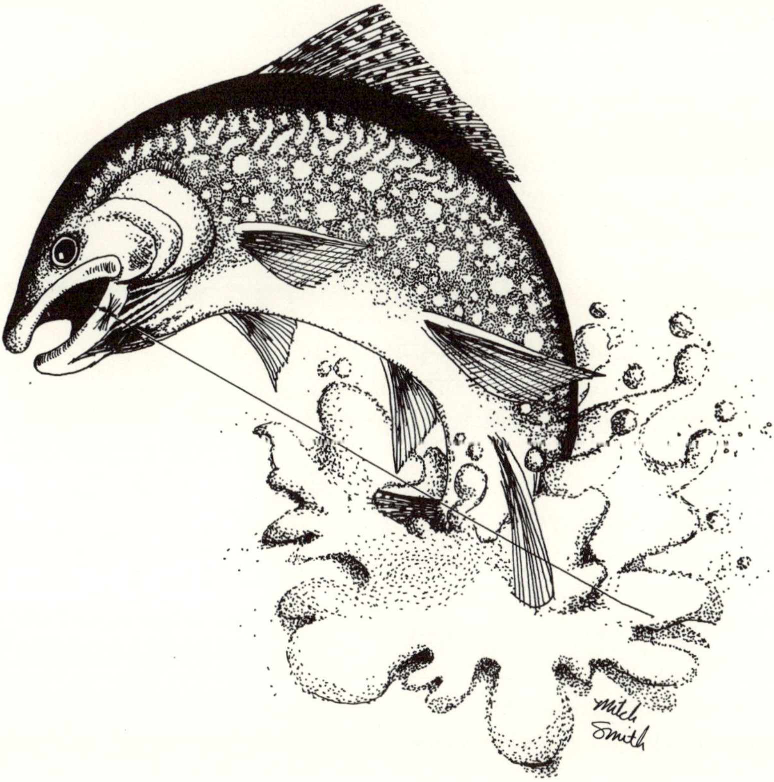

Country Lad

Country Lad, with coat of tan,
Pawn of nature's rustic plan.
Tousled hair and prankish grin,
Joys unbounded there within.
My knowledge gained from many books,
Yours from meadows, trees and brooks.
Mother Nature there to guide you,
All her beauty there beside you.

For this thing that's called success,
I'd trade it for your happiness.
Confined am I to office bare,
Your great outdoors I'd like to share.
In large cities gray and cold,
Quest for wealth make men grow old.
Daily routine, care and strife,
So different from your carefree life.

Yours the sunshine, mine the rain,
Yours the freedom, mine the pain.
Eleven months I have but dreams,
Of your forests, lakes and streams.
Of your valleys and your hills,
The evening song of whippoorwills.
Those willows, elders, lofty pine,
Forever yours – so seldom mine.

You know where the trout are biting,
Where the ripened berries are inviting.
Where the cherry blossoms grow,
Where their fragrant petals blow.
Where the bees have honeycombs,
Where the beaver build their homes.
Where blossoms grow in fairest hue,
In wooded glens the violets blue.

You're free to romp o'er daisied fields,
To breathe the fragrance clover yields.
To share your blessings, gifts of God,
To tread again where I once trod.
To live again those carefree years,
To shed myself of worldly cares.
A world of beauty, filled with joy,
Pray, enjoy it while you may, my boy.

All too soon those years have flown,
They slip away so unbeknown.
Now my short stay there must suffice,
Then back again to governed life.
But two short weeks of days sublime,
A merest sip of the rarest wine.
Seems a pity that someday you'll be,
Successful such as men like me.

My Partner

The inspiration for "My Partner" was actually heaven-sent. In many of my poems, I have written about experiences I enjoyed with my two boys, and the wonderful hours we spent together on fine trout streams in Michigan and northern Ontario. Yes, I really grew up with those two boys. It was ever a series of winter planning and summer fishing. Then along came World War II and, just as I had contemplated, both realized they had a job to perform. I'm proud to say they both volunteered for service. Lloyd, the eldest, entered the Navy, and Harold, although underage, volunteered for the Air Corps. Being underage, he was rejected then, but finally wound up with the 82nd Airborne Division. So with both boys away, I was practically living in a dream world.

I still continued fishing and hunting whenever possible, but not as frequently as when the boys were home. Then, after the war years, came college days for the boys, and finally wedding bells. By this time I realized that the boys had their own responsibilities. Those earlier days when we had spent so much time together had ended.

Those earlier days had left me with such wonderful memories that I began to wish that, by some miracle, I would be blessed with another son; to be more specific, another young fishing partner. I realized that as my wife, Dell, and I were both crowding forty, another son was practically out of the question. But from force of habit, I suppose, I would convey this message to God in my prayer each night. This went on until March 1947, when one night, as we were sitting in the living room, Dell confided to me, "I know it sounds silly, but I have all the symptoms of being pregnant."

"No!" I responded in the most feigned tone of amazement and disbelief that I could muster. "Why, that's ridiculous. You must be imagining those things."

"Perhaps so," Dell replied, "but imagination or not, those crazy symptoms are there. It's probably something to do with the change of life, so let's forget that I ever mentioned it." And for the moment, as far as Dell was concerned, the subject was dropped.

But her confession had kindled that tiny ray of hope deep in my heart which I had nourished and cherished through the years. The mere thought, however slight, of another baby on the way seemed to open a brand-new world for me. My entire soul seemed to be engulfed with a feeling of exultation and hope.

During the weeks following, my hopes had risen to towering heights. I began to realize what a terrific letdown I would experience if it turned out to be just a false alarm. After all, Dell had not mentioned anything more about it. At times I was tempted to inquire, but refrained from doing so because I was afraid of what her answer might be. That beautiful world of hopes and dreams would come crashing down about me.

Then came that wonderful moment when all my fears and anxieties were laid to rest. Dell met me at the door one evening and informed that I was about to become a father again. She had visited the doctor that day and he had confirmed her suspicions that a baby was on the way.

"When is he due to arrive?" I asked.

"What do you mean 'he'?" Dell replied. "You know it could be a girl. As far as the doctor could ascertain, it will be sometime around the middle of October. Are you surprised?"

"Surprised," I answered, "Why, I'm delighted. This is the greatest piece of news I've ever heard."

From that moment on I was living on cloud nine, counting the days, anticipating the time to come when I could take him camping and fishing. Somehow I just knew it had to be a boy, as everything had gone along so well thus far. After all, the good Lord would not send me a girl for a fishing partner. But I had also decided that if it happened to be a girl, she was going to be the greatest little tomboy that ever lived, and able to cast a fly with the best of them. Of course I hadn't mentioned anything to Dell about this, as she would probably alter my plans in a hurry.

The baby was due to arrive in 1947. That would make a span of fifteen years between the baby and my youngest girl, Patsy. I may add here that I regret not taking Patsy on more trips to the great outdoors, as she was truly a fine girl. Through the years we had enjoyed numerous trips north as a family group. On these occasions we would stay in rented cabins and cottages, usually at a lake where the kids could enjoy boating and swimming. Several times I have taken Patsy along on camping trips and she really enjoyed them, especially the trout fishing. Now, with the fleeting years, I feel rather sorry that I did not do so more often.

Then the great moment arrived October 22, 1947. The old stork had been hovering mighty close. Dell had entered the hospital at about 5 p.m. After what seemed like an eternity sitting in that hospital lobby, watching those younger fellows pace up and down the floor in their anxiety, I jumped to me feet when I saw our doctor approaching me with a grin on his face. I just about collapsed with joy when he grasped my hand and said, "Congratulations, you have a fine big baby boy." So you will understand why I say the inspiration for the following poem, "My Partner," was sent from heaven.

My Partner

I'll ever take him when I go,
To visit Mother Nature's realm,
That virgin world, that's all aglow,
Where God is always at the helm.
When another needs a helping hand,
It should always be extended,
That little guy must understand,
We must live as God intended.

For every wrong, show him the right,
Explain the pitfalls o'er life's way,
Teach him to thank God every night,
For all the blessings of the day.
Keep myself ever neat and trim,
Set a pattern for him to see,
To make a better man of him,
'Twill make a better one of me.

Your Boy

When the planning phase has ended,
And those maps are tucked away,
And the magic hour approaches,
When you'll again be on your way.
You've checked those boots and waders,
And you've checked each rod and reel,
Those sleeping bags and lanterns,
And the dip nets and the creel.

All the groceries and foodstuffs,
And you've checked the boat and tent,
The items in that tackle box,
To be sure of its content.
Yes, things seem to be in order,
But there's one thing could be wrong,
Will you leave on that vacation,
Without your boy along?

You say the lad is much too young,
That his years just number ten,
You say he has a lot to learn,
Before joining grown-up men.
No doubt he's listened as you planned,
And indulged in boyish dreams,
Then wept because he's never seen,
That great world of lakes and streams.

Yes, he's listened to your stories,
Probably lived through every one,
While looking forward to that day,
When he may partake in your fun.
All preparations have been made,
But your planning could be wrong,
If you leave on that vacation,
Without your boy along.

So ask the lad to go along,
It will make his young heart glad,
I know that he'll be mighty proud,
That he has you for a dad.
Then teach him how to bait a hook,
And the art to cast a fly,
Let him meet old Mother Nature,
With her treasures there nearby.

The proper way to set up camp,
And the knack to build a fire,
Explain the rules of sportsmanship,
The world of nature will require.
It will double your enjoyment,
Plus — less problems later on,
So why not reconstruct your plan,
And take your boy along.

Casey's Trout

The story of my greatest thrill,
In taking of a trout,
Called for so little lore or skill,
But the best beyond a doubt.
It took place on the Filer Creek,
Just above the Manistee,
And what made this one so unique,
It was Casey's first, you see.

The little tyke was barely five,
But was forever wishing,
The happy day would soon arrive,
When I would take him fishing.
'Twas the first day of September,
And conditions were ideal,
And his joys I'll long remember,
As I rigged his rod and reel.

With rubber boots and old felt
To which I had added flies,
He really looked the part at that,
And a sight for these old eyes.
'Twas but a short drive to the stream,
I had fished it once before,
And really breathed a prayer, suprem
That the little lad would score.

As we left the car I led the way,
While I kept a sharp lookout,
For a spot where my young protégé,
Might entrap a careless trout.
I spied a pool there just ahead,
Where the waters paused a bit,
The angler's voice within me said,
"Go no farther, this is it."

I cautioned Casey to be still,
As I watched him bait his hook,
The little guy was all a-thrill,
With a wild expectant look.
I waited as he moved ahead,
While I breathed a prayer, devout,
Though part of it was left unsaid,
As young Casey hooked his trout.

I heard him scream, "I've got one, Dad,"
As the fish flew through the air,
The greatest thrill I've ever had,
A moment beyond compare.
A little boy just filled with joy,
As he danced and pranced about,
That memory naught can destroy,
The epic of Casey's trout.

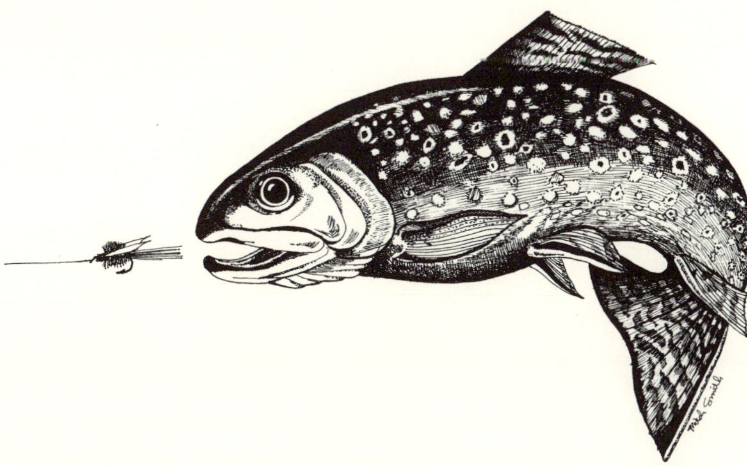

Sportsman's World

Sportsman's World

It's a magic world of splendor,
Set apart from things we know,
With a welcome for each member,
With rod or gun or bow.
It's a world of pride and honor,
And it seeks the best there is,
So, my friend, before you enter,
Be prepared these things to give:

To forget those petty jealousies,
Of the other fellow's luck,
But to grasp his hand in friendship,
If he's downed an eight-point buck.
Sincere congratulations,
To be your every wish,
And forget the thing called envy,
When he's creeled the larger fish.

To consider it your duty,
To protect each lake and stream,
Keep the forests as God made them,
Ever beautiful and clean.
Though you may have kit elaborate,
Or the poorest in the land,
You are all considered equal,
In this sportsman's world so grand.

You are strictly on your honor,
As you wander far and near,
So leave a trail you're proud of,
With nothing there to fear.
To be worry free of wardens,
You may meet from time to time,
For you'll derive much satisfaction,
To uphold their standards fine.

Remember that your actions,
Are watched by others, too,
For a hundred thousand sportsmen,
All have their eyes on you.
To reminisce, on winter's nights,
On the good things you have done,
To have old Mother Nature,
Be proud to call you son.

Dedicated to the outdoor sportsman's clubs throughout the nation, and to the many fine members of the Dearborn Woods and Waters Club of Dearborn, Michigan

In Nature's Realm

I'm tired of reading headlines,
Of sinister things that loom,
Of watching far horizons,
'Neath the constant clouds of gloom.
Of hydrogens and atoms,
And talk of impending doom,
Thank God there is another world,
Where these subjects find no room –
In nature's realm.

I'm tired of reading headlines,
Of the failures of man,
Of the everlasting struggle,
All across our worldly span.
Where the thought of brotherhood,
Enters not into his plan,
Thank God there is another world,
All devoid of hate and sham –
In nature's realm.

A world where men are equal,
Be he barefoot boy or king,
Equipped in finest raiment,
Or just willow branch and string.
With forests, lakes and rivers,
Where the songbirds always sing,
A world of priceless treasures,
Without fee for anything –
In nature's realm.

A Sportsman

One who enjoys the lakes and streams,
In all their natural beauty,
To protect their crystal waters,
He regards a sacred duty.
All those wondrous things of nature,
He will try to understand,
He's the measure of a sportsman,
And the yardstick of a man.

Protects the forests beautiful,
While there on a woodland hike,
Taking every care and caution,
With that match and pipe.
Sees those campfires are extinguished,
Leaves his campsite spic and span,
He's the measure of a sportsman,
And the yardstick of a man.

When those startled deer start running,
Whether they be fast or slow,
He will never press the trigger,
If his target be a doe.
Devoted to his fellowman,
He's so loyal and partisan,
That's the measure of a sportsman,
And the yardstick of a man.

Illegal fish, or undersize,
He returns to lake or brook,
Using every care and caution,
While removing from the hook.
For to aid in conservation,
He will do the best he can,
That's the measure of a sportsman,
And the yardstick of a man.

He's a friend of all game wardens,
As there's nothing he must hide,
And to any legal trophies,
He'll display with joy and pride.
In that great world of rod and gun,
He's both prince and nobleman,
He's the measure of a sportsman,
And the yardstick of a man.

Seasons

Good old spring is here again,
With fresh March winds and April rain.
It seems to be an old, old story,
Hailing spring in all its glory.
I'll admit it's mighty nice,
To see the end of snow and ice.
But then I claim so many reasons,
Why we should love those other seasons.

Take summertime that's on the way,
A season when all folks are gay.
Picnics, hikes and swell vacations,
It's summertime for recreations.
Flowers, crops and fruits have birth,
In those alone it proves its worth.
It then bows out in all its splendor,
But leaves us dreams to long remember.

Then autumn with its scenery rare,
Is like a jewel beyond compare.
With a thousand hues it paints the trees,
Then changes them with gentle breeze.
The fields it paints with golden grain,
With autumn suns and gentle rains.
At times I'd vote to name the fall,
The greatest season of them all.

Autumn ends and winter's here,
With its days so crisp and clear.
The air is filled with crystal snows,
In ermine white all things repose.
Winter sports are so much fun,
With joy and thrills for everyone.
Old Jack Frost brings cheer and health,
That can't be bought with man-made wealth.

So we should thank the Lord above,
For all these seasons that we love.
For the different seasons which He sends,
Each has much to recommend.
For the joys and pleasures He has sent,
To make our life on earth content.
Spring, summer, winter, fall –
Thanks, dear God, we love them all.

Vacation Time

A great event begins today,
That fills my heart with cheer,
It's something I've looked forward to,
Each day throughout the year.
It's something I've provided for,
A little every pay,
Vacation time has now arrived,
Yes, it begins today.

I try to be so nonchalant,
And take it all in stride,
But I feel so doggone happy,
I'm all pent up inside.
The kids are telling all their friends,
And mother seems so gay,
I hope the neighbors understand,
That it begins today.

For when a man has punched a clock,
Each day the whole year through,
And toiled inside the same old shop,
There with the same old crew.
Just working on the same old job,
Don't fault me when I say,
That I'm feeling mighty happy,
That it begins today.

I've put the car in first-class shape,
Been working on it nights,
Added many extra gadgets,
And checked the brakes and lights.
I've changed the oil and filled the tank,
We'll soon be on our way,
The old bus seems to understand,
Vacation starts today.

And mother, too, has worked so hard,
To get the things all set,
And says to me, "Remind me, John,
If something I forget."
She has all the clothes so spic and span,
And neatly put away,
She seems relieved the time has come,
And it begins today.

Throughout the year we've talked about,
The places where we'd go,
A hundred calls I know were planned,
On friends we used to know.
If we made the briefest visit,
Just to pass the time of day,
We simply could not see them all,
When we begin today.

So mother plans to visit,
The girls to ski and swim,
While their brother wants some fishing,
I'll have to humor him.
They've all decided what they'll do,
In these two weeks of play,
I know they'll keep me on the go,
When it begins today.

But I'm mighty glad to do it,
If only for their sake,
For I know when it has ended,
How these old bones will ache.
A man should have a week at least,
To recuperate, I say.
And to rest up when it's over,
But it just begins today.

Johnny Buck

Let me digress from my favorite subject of trout fishing for a few lines on another subject close to my heart: the beautiful deer herd of Michigan.

I'll admit I'm not much of a deer hunter because, for some unknown reason, I'd much rather miss my quarry than bring him down or, better yet, use a movie camera in place of a gun. I cannot explain my reason for this. It may be that I dislike the idea of dressing them out, or the task of hauling them out of the woods. I realize that a certain number of deer should be taken each year in order to keep the herd in balance. If this were not the case, the herd would grow to such great proportions that thousands of them would be dying of starvation, and nothing could be more cruel. So perhaps it might be better to attribute my reason for feeling this way to laziness.

Through the years it has been my pleasure to see hundreds of these beautiful animals, mostly during summer months while camped by a lake or stream. Somehow they never become commonplace to me, as I still get the same thrill as I watch them gracefully glide over stumps and other obstacles in their path, or perhaps pause to watch me from a ridge overlooking a stream.

Many summer evenings we have driven along the back roads, constantly on the lookout for them, trusting that it may be our good fortune to focus them in the lens of a camera.

One evening while indulging in this favorite pastime, my partner and I spotted three beautiful does on a rise within two hundred feet from the car. We paused to watch them, and my partner whispered, "I'll bet you anything that there's a buck back in those poplars behind them. Let's wait until they move." The wind must have been in the right direction, as they did not notice us in the car that was almost concealed from their view. Sure enough, just as they began to move out across the clearing, a beautiful buck emerged from the trees and followed them.

They were truly a sight to see. Besides making that deer spotting trip a huge success, they supplied the inspiration for the following poem, "Johnny Buck."

Johnny Buck

Now Johnny Buck was a ten point buck,
A beautiful sight to see,
'Twas the whispered word throughout the herd,
There was none as smart as he.
It was no surprise that he had three wives,
Three beautiful graceful does,
And he'd flout his luck to his fellow buck,
Wherever he chanced to go.

As they paused to rest on a hilly crest,
He boasted to them one day,
"You're a lucky three to be with me,
I'm monarch of all I survey."
Then Jane would say in her wistful way,
"Now, Johnny, stop your bragging,"
Though his pride was hurt, his reply was curt –
"Janie, you're always nagging."

"Do I lead you wrong when the hunt is on,
And show you the safest spots,
Where the cedars stand in dense swampland,
So far from the hunters' shots?
And I also know where the acorns grow,
Atop of yon oak-treed hill,
Where you ladies fine may safely dine,
And oft-times have ate your fill."

"But," said Betsy Doe, "I'd like to know,
Why you ever stay behind us?
You should lead the way to those spots you say,
Where hunters will never find us."
Johnny answered, "Well, this I should not tell,
But to make you ladies happy,
'Twas a trick taught me as a boy, you see,
By a very wise old pappy.

"Be ever alert and you'll not get hurt,
For you know that I'm nearby,
Though I'm in the rear, please have no fear,
For you're 'neath my watchful eye."
And there were days as they'd browse and graze,
Johnny Buck to them has turned,
Like a wise old sage from another age,
To brief them on things he'd learned.

"When you find salt blocks in stumps and rocks,
Regard them with utmost fear,
For they're placed by men, the vilest men,
Who will fire as you draw near.
You haven't a chance with these poaching scamps,
So you must respect and fear them,
For a longer life, take my advice,
Keep moving and don't go near them."

As they paused one night a great beam of light,
Seemed to hold them mesmerized,
As they watched appalled, transfixed, enthralled,
And completely terrorized.
Johnny saw with fright their tragic plight,
And called from the shadows there –
"Quick, run girls, run, they may have a gun,
And I have no wives to spare."

They turned as one and began to run,
As they never had run before,
They had no desire to draw the fire,
And perhaps let a poacher score.
With his perfect rack laid o'er his back,
Johnny called to the leading doe –
"Janie, change your course, keep bearing north,
We'll be safer there, I know."

Propelled by fear those beautiful deer,
Sped on swiftly through the night,
'Twas a sight to see for naught could be,
More picturesque in flight.
With all danger past, they paused at last,
Crowding close to Johnny Buck,
And he felt real good, as a husband should,
Who appreciates such luck.

Said he, "Let us rest, I think it best,
While deciding what to do,
It was quite a scare we had back there,
And an ordeal to go through.
You may have no fear for this section here,
Was favored by my mother,
A vast timberland where tall trees stand,
With loads of food and cover."

But Patsy said, as she turned her head,
"Is that not a highway there?
See those lights which pierce the night,
With that eerie, frightening glare."
Johnny studied, too, and replied, "'Tis true,
Man has arrived before us,
Ever clearing land for their highways grand,
Leaving very little for us."

"With their taverns, bars and lines of cars,
And the lilt of their ribald song,
Where flashing signs have replaced the pines,
In a world where we don't belong."
"But," said Janie Doe, "As ever north we go,
Just where is this promised land,
With an era born, where we raise our fawn,
Without the constant fear of man?"

Johnny bowed his head as he sadly said,
"There's little distance left, I fear,
So let's make the best of what there's left,
With the Great Lakes' shoreline near.
But, girls, cheer up, for with Johnny Buck,
You should all be gay and happy,
For outwit I can the thing called man,
With the tricks I learned from pappy.

"So let us roam o'er our wilderness home,
Like the buffalo of yesteryear,
'Til ousted by man in their greedy plan,
Then we, too, shall disappear."

The Deer Hunters

Bid him, "Good-bye," with a cheer, not a sigh,
And just throw in an extra kiss;
He'll go anyway, so why not be gay?
For harsh words here are strictly amiss.
With their car loaded down, the guys head from town,
With their rifles, red jackets and hoods;
To again ply their luck, with the fast running buck,
Away back in the vast north woods.

Far off the main road, they stop and unload,
And hastily set up their camp;
They then squat around, on the cold frosty ground,
Munch lunch by a gasoline lamp.
They'll crawl out at dawn, from a sack nice and warm,
And dress in the damp, frigid air;
They don't mind the snow, being anxious you know,
To drive that big buck from his lair.

The eggs and the ham, left too long in the pan,
Are scorched slightly, to say the least;
But at old breakfast call, they smile one and all,
And really enjoy the feast.
Then comes that long hike, to a spot they all like,
For stalking those beautiful deer;
The temperature's low, with cold winds and snow,
But not a complaint do you hear.

On a deer run at dawn, where most heroes are born,
One lights up his pipe to relax;
While his buddies will romp, through snow in the
    swamp,
All watching for deer signs or tracks.
Being lucky that day, they drove one his way,
And made him a sad disbeliever;
For he emptied his gun, as he watched that deer run,
And got him a case of buck fever.

Far into the night, he recalls with delight,
Those great episodes of the day;
Deploring his luck, with six shots in that buck,
And the doggone thing still got away.
They have run out of ham, and are fed up with spam,
Dream of camp meat that no one has shot;
And the menu at times, nothing like Duncan Hines,
Getting by on what little they've got.

And thus the week goes, with its joys and its woes,
And no doubt some fellows are looking;
To that journey back home, where Mom waits alone,
To partake in her good home cooking.
And so the hunt ends, they all part as friends,
With some comforting words of cheer;
But one thing is certain, as down comes the curtain,
They'll be right back for more next year.

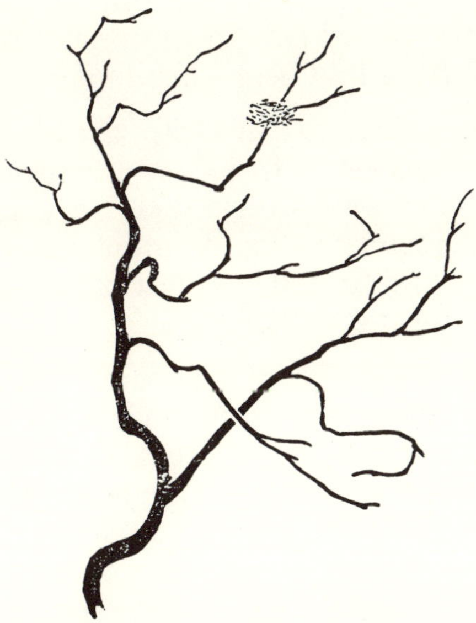

The Aging Trapper

Here is another of my favorite poems, inspired by a rather interesting discussion I had with an elderly gentleman I became acquainted with one day up in Northern Ontario.

This took place in July 1949. Our party included my two sons, Lloyd and Harold, and our friend and fishing partner, Clayton Bills. We had made several previous trips to this rugged country in quest of trout. We had enjoyed those trips so much, that once again we found ourselves in complete agreement to sally forth in quest of that lunker of which all trout men seem to dream. The long drive there and back, for a mere week of fishing, appeared to be the only deterrent, but visions of those big ones waiting there at the end of the road decided the issue.

Our trip on this occasion was uneventful and, as our knowledge of the area was very limited, we decided that once again we would set up camp on Northland Lake where the fishing had been excellent.

Monday, our first day in camp, the weather was cool and the sky overcast. After several hours of fishing the stream which ran out of the lake, we had managed to creel about a dozen nice trout among us. We enjoyed an early supper, and talked over our plans for the morrow around the evening campfire.

When we crawled out of our sleeping bags the following morning, we discovered a steady drizzle of rain. Thus we spent the entire day in camp, where we passed the time working on our gear, playing quite a number of sessions of euchre and cribbage, and reading. Although the weather was so miserable, it did not dampen our spirits too much, as we found this forced rest period very welcome after the long drive. We figured that tomorrow we would surely make up for lost time.

Upon arising Wednesday morning, we were greeted by that same old rain with the sky completely overcast, anything but trout fishing weather. One day of rain during a week of trout fishing is a blessing in disguise, but then two or more days of rain is somewhat of a catastrophe and usually ruins the entire week. Here we were sitting around in the tent while those precious hours were slipping away.

Midday and still no let up in the rain. By this time discouragement was beginning to assert itself. I prepared lunch and, while we were sitting around munching sandwiches and bemoaning our ill luck, Clay came up with a suggestion that we go for a drive to explore the countryside a bit and break the monotony. We all agreed it was an excellent idea.

While driving along a gravel road in the direction of the town of Searchmont, we came upon a beautiful rustic cabin located on top of a hill by the road. Alongside the cabin was quite a waterfall where a stream came cascading down over the rocks from the high land above. By this time the rain had let up a little, and Clay pulled off the road so that we might have more time to enjoy this beautiful setting. It then occurred to me that the residents of this cabin would surely have a vast knowledge of the surrounding countryside. As the boys had gone down to look the stream over, I walked up to the cabin and rapped on the door.

Here I became acquainted with the gentleman who inspired this poem. He greeted me most affably and invited me in. Even though I had been impressed with the rustic beauty of the cabin and waterfall from the road, I was even more impressed with the interior. I was particularly intrigued with the furnishings, as all the contents seemed to fit in and beautifully match the rugged countryside which surrounded it.

Racks of antlers on the walls, a large rack above an old stone fireplace being just about perfect, a huge easy chair which had been carved out of a solid tree trunk, several handmade lamps, a large bear skin rug stretched before the firplace, and many other items created an atmosphere of adventure and memories. It was a setting which appeared to stem from the creation of an artist's brush.

My genial host, although getting along in years, appeared to fit perfectly in this rustic setting. Tall but unbowed, greying of hair but with a twinkle in his eye, he made a fellow feel perfectly at home in his presence. We sat there and chatted about many things pertaining to this country: lakes and streams which might be reached by car, species of fish to be found therein, and information which seemed to be priceless if a fellow only had sufficient time to put it all to use. I just sat there and listened intrigued as he began recalling some of his early experiences in and around that rugged countryside. Even as he talked I could somehow sense an echo of regret in his voice, seeming to lament the fact that in recent years he had slowed down a little. Aging is a frightening thought for all of us. I believe those fellows who derive so much pleasure and adventure found out-of-doors have an added concern.

No doubt the thought has occurred to you, too, as you have sat by the campfire, or while wading a favorite stream. In situations such as this it's rather a frightening thought that the day will arrive when you can no longer indulge in these heart-warming adventures.

So with these thoughts in mind, is it any wonder why I was able to decipher a tone of lament in that elderly gentleman's voice as I sat there and listened that day? Yes, he reluctantly admitted that he had slowed down a little, but seemed unable to find a reason for so doing. It was a discussion to long remember. It was while mulling over certain parts of that interesting conversation during the weeks following that I wrote, "The Aging Trapper."

The Aging Trapper

Not gettin' the pelts like I used to get 'em,
Can't remember the traps or just where I set 'em,
Mind's gettin' jest a bit hazy, I reckon,
I jest can't figure it out.

The mornin's seem colder and wetter the dew,
Though I bundle up more the dampness goes through,
And I find that the hills are a bit steeper too,
I jest can't figure it out.

It seems a bit further when makin' the rounds,
And harder to separate those forest sounds,
Been cuppin' my ear for the bay of the hounds,
I jest can't figure it out.

Jest can't seem to pick out the buck from the doe,
Either they're runnin' faster or I'm a mite slow,
Seems I'm not as fast with a rifle or bow,
I jest can't figure it out.

Streams seem more brushy and faster the water,
Not gettin' distance on casts that I ought-a,
When I squint at the time the old arm seems shorter,
I jest can't figure it out.

Been havin' more trouble to tie on a fly,
The leader seems thicker and smaller the eye,
Seems I'm doin' more squintin' each time I try,
I jest can't figure it out.

Not shavin' as often as I used to do,
It's gettin' to be an ordeal to go through,
The mirror I use seems a bit cloudy too,
I jest can't figure it out.

I feel like a fool when the boys come from town,
An' miss lots of laughs when they act up and clown,
Seems I doze off to sleep each time I sit down,
I jest can't figure it out.

A Sportsman's Thanksgiving

As frost creeps o'er the forest floor,
And a chill is in the air,
With a myriad of colors,
In the woodlands everywhere.
A light shines in the window,
Of a cabin in the glen,
And gathered 'round the fireplace,
There's a group of happy men.

Reliving cherished memories,
Reminiscing, one by one,
Recalling rare adventures,
With the rod and bow and gun.
There are trophies o'er the mantle,
There's a bearskin on the floor,
And I realized the many things,
We had to be thankful for.

Days in the snow-clad forests,
As we stalked the wary deer,
And the tense anticipation,
As a fine specimen draws near.
The splashing of a rainbow,
As it leaps to take a fly,
And the song of rippling waters,
Reflecting colors of the sky.

The drumming of a partridge,
When his mating time's at hand,
The unmatched natural beauty,
Where the virgin timber stands.
The colors of the ringneck,
As he rises from the swale,
The stillness of a pointer,
As he pauses on the trail.

When the ducks glide in formation,
As the circle to alight,
And the working of retrievers,
What a truly stirring sight.
A campsite at the dawning,
With those fishing creels and rods,
And the coffee there a-perkin',
Like the nectar of the gods.

There's the scent of pine logs burnin',
As the evenin' shadows fall,
With sessions 'round the campfire,
Just the greatest of them all.
We owe the Lord a heap o' thanks,
For this land in which we're living,
I trust these lines convey to Him,
A sportsman's true thanksgiving.

The Rape of the Forest

I decided that my book would not be complete without a few lines dedicated to those romantic lumbering days when I was a boy. After I was dismissed from school I would hike back to the timberline to watch the lumberjacks at work cutting the towering pines. It was fascinating to watch those giant trees come crashing to the earth, and see the dispatch displayed in the trimming and loading. I can also recall many scoldings I received upon arriving home too late for the evening meal.

But even as the cutting and loading of the timber were so fascinating to me, the river drives were even more so. On several occasions I dared to miss school in order to watch the log drivers working like trojans with cant hook and peavey, endeavoring to release the dreaded jams. Many times I watched as one of those men was thrown into the swirling waters when the logs suddenly began to move. At other times the drivers would ride a single log to a point of safety. Those fellows were as agile as cats.

One of my greatest thrills was the time I was hired by one of the camp cooks to deliver lunches to the men along the river. The lunches would be made up, tied in cloth, then strung on a long pole. A friend and I would hike down the river with this pole on our shoulders and pass them out to the drivers along the way. None of these fellows was lacking in appetite. It seemed to me there was sufficient food in one of those bundles to feed a horse. Regardless of this, many drivers would insist on taking two of them. This would really rile up the cooks, but there was little we kids could do about it. Personally, it was all right with us as it made the load lighter and the hike much shorter. We were paid the princely sum of fifteen cents per trip plus a meal back at camp; not a great deal of money for the time involved, but sufficient to make us feel we were part of a great operation.

Yes, it was truly a wonderful experience. Please join me in a hike back along memory trail to that era of lumbering days in old Quebec.

The Rape of the Forest

Hark to the hiss of the crosscut,
Shrill is the cut of the blade,
The spewing of chips and sawdust,
As numerous inroads are made.
The great timberline receding,
Before the onslaught of man,
Taking, but never returning,
Forgive, Lord, their one-way plan.

Never so much as a seedling,
Which might blossom forth and grow,
And bring on a stand of timber,
Like their heritage long ago.
Hark now, the shout of, "Timber,"
A byword to rape and rob,
Cuttings left to parch in the sun,
For fires to finish the job.

Again, there's the shout of, "Timber,"
Thunderous crash of the pine,
Re-echoing a thousand times,
All along that timberline.
The straining of those stalwart teams,
The arching of froth-flecked manes,
Obeying every cursed command,
Fighting there 'neath those tightened reins.

Now gradually inching forward,
See those great loads pitch and sway,
Along that rutted, winding trail,
To where the frozen river lay.
'Neath the urge of hook and peavey,
By those rugged lumbermen,
Stacked to await the winter's end,
Before they'll move on again.

When the ice has left the rivers,
Their journey resumes once more,
Cascading down those hilly banks,
Trailing those legions gone before.

Springtime Challenge

Signs of plant life breaking through,
    God once more sends all things new;
Sends the songbirds back to sing,
    Tells one and all that this is spring.
Changes all things far and wide,
    Scars of yesteryear to hide;
Adorns the trees in leafy gowns,
    With grassy carpet all around.

Flowers raise their heads to pray,
    And glorify with colors gay;
The world is cleansed in springtime splendor,
    God's gift to all, His heart is tender.
Seems like a challenge from the sky,
    To mortal men like you and I;
Another chance to start anew,
    And rectify the things we do.

Your Spouse

"Your Spouse" is a little poem I jotted down regarding one of life's grim tragedies; a tragedy which could happen to any man who might blunder into it with his eyes closed.

I refer to that very congenial young fellow who used to accompany you whenever possible on those jaunts to the great outdoors. All you had to do was mention that you were planning on a pheasant hunt or a few days of trout fishing, and this young chap was ready to go. In all probability you have met him, too. He may even have been one of your buddies. From the moment the trip is decided on, he begins checking over his gear to be sure that everything is in tip-top shape. Yes, he just seems to live for those wonderful days in the woods.

He's that type of a fellow who can't seem to do enough around camp, a regular clown during campfire sessions. For a young fellow, he's really mastered the art of raising trout. Woe be to the pheasant that carelessly rises from the swale within range of his gun. He's really a great guy to have along as he fits into the picture so naturally.

But then along comes romance and tragedy. He's finally discovered that dream girl. A whirlwind romance begins, and you wind up with an invitation to the wedding. Of course, you feel happy about the whole thing. Until the wedding night when you manage to get him off to one side and inquire whether his bride will approve of those jaunts to that world of hunting and fishing. You feel a chill run up and down your spine when he replies, "Well, to tell you the truth, I really forgot to ask her. But I'm sure she will approve."

Well, on the majority of occasions they will approve and live happily ever after, especially when she agrees to go along and learns to enjoy it. But tragedy enters the picture when the little woman puts her foot down and cites any number of reasons why he should not even suggest going with the boys on these occasions; such as those chores around the house which never seem to end or a Sunday visit at her mother's. In fact, she never seems to run out of excuses as to why he shouldn't go. The final chapter in this very sad story occurs when that treasured gear — those guns and the fishing equipment — is stored away in some remote corner to gather dust with the wings of time.

Therefore, may I suggest to those young fellows who may be nearing the threshold of matrimony, those fellows who have a yen for hunting and fishing. Endeavor to find out before it's too late just what her feelings are on this extremely important subject. Then make your final plans from that point. For once you say "yes," you have reached the point of no return.

Your Spouse

You know, brother, you're in heaven,
If you have wed an outdoor girl;
When vacation days and weekends,
Are ever one big happy whirl.
And, too, you're very fortunate,
If she will only go along;
Deciding if you like that life,
To disapprove would be so wrong.

And consider yourself lucky,
If she agrees to let you go;
To that peaceful world which you love,
But one she does not care to know.
Then again, your're fairly lucky,
If she okays a week or two;
And allows her quiet reluctance,
To recede in her love for you.

But if she's very definite,
And quite emphatically says, "No;"
With your lifetime spent a-dreamin',
Of places you desire to go.
To lakes and stream and wooded glens,
But you never have the chance, sir;
The opposite to the first line,
Of this ditty spells the answer.

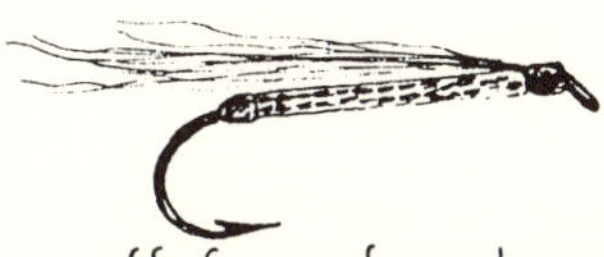
black nose dace, streamer

Postlude

We Thank Thee, Lord

We thank Thee, Lord, for springtime,
And the splendor o'er the land,
For the freshness and the beauty,
Which respond to your command.
For the fragrance of the blossoms,
And the budding leaf unfurled,
Accept the heartfelt gratitude,
Of this undeserving world.

We thank Thee, Lord, for summer,
And the seedlings' gentle birth,
As in answer to your bidding,
They emerge from mother earth.
For the blossoms of the orchards,
Now awakened by your hand,
Accept the heartfelt gratitude,
Of this undeserving land.

We thank Thee, Lord, for autumn,
For those fields of green and gold,
For the beauty of the woodlands,
As those dazzling hues unfold.
For the bounty of the harvest,
As your gracious gift to man,
Accept the heartfelt gratitude,
Of this undeserving clan.

We thank Thee, Lord, for winter,
With the world of nature sleeping,
There 'neath a cloak of ermine white,
A rendezvous they're keeping.
The longer nights, the fireside bright,
The peal of bell in steeple,
Accept the heartfelt gratitude
Of an undeserving people.

About the Author

The following are excerpts from the author's autobiographical recollections, recorded in a story entitled *Sonny Jones.* In it he writes about the early days of his life, which began on the day after Christmas in 1903.

My heritage at birth was a passionate fondness for the great outdoors, which through the years has become an obsession with me. Let me start at the beginning and relate the circumstances surrounding my birth. My parents and Emily, my only sister, migrated from England early in the twentieth century, booking passage on the S. S. Sicilian bound for Montreal, Canada. From what I have been able to piece together, they were practically destitute, but hopeful about beginning a new life in a young and growing country.

During the voyage up the St. Lawrence River towards Montreal, while travelling through a heavy fog, the liner came to grief when it ran aground on a sand bar. After many fruitless hours during which tugboats tried to free the liner, it was decided that in order to lighten the load, passengers would be put ashore at a place known as Penticoast. It was here that my parents contracted employment in a sawmill. They were then transported to Lost River, Quebec where the mill was located.

Dad was put to work as a teamster, and Mother as a cook. There in Lost River I was born some seven months later. I am at a loss to know just who took care of mother during delivery or even whether there was a doctor in this remote section of the country. I do not believe that my birth was ever registered, for although I have tried on many occasions to obtain a copy of my birth certificate, I have been unable to do so.

It was there, far back in the forests of old Quebec, that I first saw the light of day. It was a beautiful country dotted with lakes and streams, and surrounded by tall pines. The everlasting ring of the flashing blade and the eternal grind of the cross-cut were evidence of the lumbermen moving slowly through this rustic world of virgin timber.

My parents spent almost two years in Lost River, working at very menial labor in order to accumulate sufficient funds to move on to something better. No doubt it required a great deal of ambition and fortitude on their part in order to accomplish that goal.

In August 1905, having saved enough money to purchase a horse and rig, my parents decided to move. Dad accepted the old horse as part of his pay, and the rig happened to be a two-seated buggy, rather the worse for wear. In this contraption they loaded their few worldly possessions and some supplies for the trip, and began their trek through the woods towards the village of Brownsburg. Brownsburg was a small picturesque village with a population of about 500. I imagine that journey must have been quite an ordeal in itself, with Mother having to care for two babies under the most primitive conditions.

Dad had chosen Brownsburg as his destination because an ammunition factory located there provided a good opportunity for employment. We settled in a small log cabin situated at the top of a hill approaching the village. I don't know whether Dad actually built the cabin or purchased it, but I know that it was rustic. Only upon reflection later in life do I remember the log cabin as being picturesque. It was built in a maple forest and surrounded by patches of spring flowers — tiger lilies, violets, and lilies of the valley.

Brownsburg had very severe winters with snow drifts so high that Dad would have to crawl out the attic window in order to clear the snow away from the doors below. The pathways to the outhouses were much like tunnels through the snow. Many times the pump was frozen solid, so Dad would melt snow and bring the water to a boil on the old box stove to thaw out the pump. On long winter evenings, Mother and Dad sat by the stove reading the newspaper, which I suppose was several days old by the time they received it. Emily and I would scrape the heavy frost off the window to watch the kids pass on their way to school, which was a short distance down the road from our cabin.

In later years I occasionally visited the old cabin, which remained untenanted after we left. In 1921, while on leave from the Canadian Army, I journeyed to the homesite. There was nothing left of the cabin, just underbrush covering the spot where it once stood. Several times during the visit I heard the hill on which it stood referred to as "Jones Hill." I was proud to learn that our name was still associated with that beautiful spot.

But I am wandering from my story. Dad was successful in obtaining employment at the ammunition factory in Brownsburg. We lived in the small cabin until I was eight years of age. Then we moved to a larger home just north of the village. Here we had plenty of garden space and raised all our own vegetables.

Fruit grew in abundance; all one had to do was pick it. During the fruit seasons we spent the majority of our spare time gathering it. This task was assigned to Emily and me, while Mother spent considerable time preserving it for the winter months ahead. Although I disliked the menial task of gathering fruit, I had no

> choice. Mother was very strict and it meant a whipping were we to return without a fair showing for our efforts. The only enjoyment I derived from it was the opportunity to visit the different sections where the fruit was found and to partake in the fine lunches Mother would prepare for us.
>
> By this time my fondness for the outdoors had begun to assert itself. Whenever possible I would spend my time hiking through the woods, building camps out of evergreen boughs, carving out bows and arrows, and endeavoring to figure out contraptions to trap small game such as squirrels and chipmunks. Although I never succeeded in trapping anything, it was worlds of fun trying.

During his boyhood, Harry spent most of his time outdoors, receiving his formal education in a small two-room schoolhouse. In his own words:

> I lived the Huckleberry Finn life of a village boy. Brownsburg at that time was one of the wonder spots of old Quebec, with an abundance of lakes and streams. In this paradise I spent my boyhood — fishing and swimming during the summer months, skiing, sledding and snowshoeing during the beautiful winters. I was known to the townsfolk in those days as mischievous "Sonny" Jones.

At the age of sixteen, Harry Jones looked for adventure and enlisted in the Canadian Army. Although he was underage, he persuaded the recruiting sergeant that he was eighteen years old, but looked young for his age. Harry joined the cavalry division of the Princess Pats regiment and was stationed in Winnipeg. Although he liked the idea of riding, he discovered he spent more time behind the horse than on top of it. As a result, he transferred to the infantry regiment where he served four years with this distinguished military unit.

After his first enlistment, Harry faced the same problem as many thousands of other servicemen returning home in the early 1920s: There was no work. So it was back to the army for him, but not for long. It is while serving his second enlistment that Harry met Delphia Oldfield and married her in 1925. Army wages could not support a couple of newlyweds, so after a few months, Harry obtained his discharge.

There is probably no way of really knowing when Harry Edward Jones first got interested in writing down his "philosophy" in poetic form, but it seems reasonable to assume that Harry certainly recalled his army days when he put those thoughts down on paper. In fact some of his most compelling poems depict the horror and the glory of conflict. "The History of the Second World War," a narrative that opens *Rhymes of a Common Man,* is the longest and most powerful of Harry's works.

Harry and Delphia were married between wars, and shared each other's lives for 57 years. As parents, they raised three sons and two daughters. In their early years, the young Jones family found itself bouncing around from town to town. First to Hamilton, Ontario where Harry worked for the Firestone Tire Company. Then on to Toronto where Harry served on the city police force. When they finally moved to Detroit, they became U.S. citizens and Harry found work with the Packer Motor Company.

However, with the Great Depression in full force, it was a period of uncertainty. Harry was in and out of work and finally had to resign himself to doing odd jobs such as washing windows and unloading coal trucks for $2 a day. He then went to work at the Penington Furniture Company for about five years: delivering furniture during the day and working as a salesman for the company at night.

In his early 30s, Harry landed a job at the J. L. Hudson Company as a driver. He would remain on this job for the next 30 years.

It was all during this time that Harry wrote his poems based on experience, observation, and the world he knew and loved. He wrote about the delights of boyhood, the beauty of Michigan, the wonder of nature, and the joy of being a sportsman. In his youth he especially enjoyed hockey and fishing. Later he would coach hockey in the army, and both coach and play for the J. L. Hudson team. He was a long-time member of the Dearborn Woods and Waters Club of Dearborn, Michigan, and served as the club's vice president.

Harry died in Detroit, Michigan on March 28, 1982, at the age of 79. May his works provide enjoyment to his readers for many years to come.